Issues in Focus

The Debate Over Genetically Engineered Food

Healthy or Harmful?

Kathiann M. Kowalski

Enslow Publishers, Inc.

40 Industrial Road   PO Box 38
Box 398   Aldershot
Berkeley Heights, NJ 07922   Hants GU12 6BP
USA   UK

http://www.enslow.com

This book is dedicated to my daughter, Laura Meissner.

Copyright © 2002 by Kathiann M. Kowalski

Library of Congress Cataloging-in-Publication Data

Kowalski, Kathiann M., 1955–
    The debate over genetically engineered food : healthy or harmful? / Kathiann M. Kowalski.
        p. cm. — (Issues in Focus)
    Includes bibliographical references and index.
    ISBN 0-7660-1686-2
    1. Genetically modified foods—Juvenile literature. [1. Genetic engineering. 2. Food—Biotechnology. 3. Agricultural biotechnology.] I. Title. II. Issues in focus (Hillside, N.J.)
    TP248.65.F66 K69   2002
    363.19'29—dc21

                                        2001006086

Printed in the United States of America

10 9 8 7 6 5 4 3 2 1

To Our Readers:
We have done our best to make sure all Internet Addresses in this book were active and appropriate when we went to press. However, the author and the publisher have no control over and assume no liability for the material available on those Internet sites or on other Web sites they may link to. Any comments or suggestions can be sent by e-mail to comments@enslow.com or to the address on the back cover.

Illustration Credits: Greenpeace, p. 6; Kathiann M. Kowalski, pp. 36, 76, 80, 87, 91; Monsanto Corp., pp. 12, 41, 64; U.S. Department of Agriculture, pp. 18, 32, 45, 50, 61, 71, 100.

Cover Illustration: U.S. Department of Agriculture. Shown is a hybrid of corn and eastern gamagrass.

Contents

Acknowledgments

The author gratefully acknowledges the assistance and insights she received from the following people and groups: John Finer, David Francis, Joseph Kovach, Katy Larkin, Ian Sheldon, and Suzanne Steel at Ohio State University; Susan Gemmell and Cim Nunn with Greenpeace Canada; Adrianne Massey of A. Massey and Associates; Lisa Dry at the Biotechnology Industry Organization; Craig Culp and Charles Margulis at Greenpeace USA; Alan McHughen at the University of Saskatchewan; Bryan Hurley of Monsanto Company; the Agricultural Research Service Photo Unit of the U.S. Department of Agriculture; Mark and Matthew Goins; Amy Naughton; and Bethany, Chris, Laura, and Michael Meissner.

Food Fights

A giant ear of corn stood guard outside the Convention on Biological Diversity in Montreal, Canada. With bloodshot eyes and jagged teeth, its angry face glared at passersby. Nearby, an activist from the environmental organization Greenpeace held a banner: "STOP GENETIC POLLUTION! BIOSAFETY NOW."[1]

Scientists came from around the world to the January 2000 conference. Among other things, they wanted to explore new ways to improve food crops. Protesters like the Greenpeace member came too. They

Activists from Greenpeace, accompanied by a sixteen-foot-tall cob of corn, demonstrate against genetically modified foods at the Convention on Biological Diversity in Montreal in January 2000.

wanted to show that they object to some of those foods.

The giant corn ear protested farmers' use of a specific type of corn. The corn was genetically engineered. In other words, the chemical code that determines the plant's genetic traits was changed. Scientists had put in genes from another species. Other terms for genetically engineered are "genetically modified," "GM," "genetically altered," and "transgenic." Genetic engineering is part of biotechnology. Biotechnology is the manipulation of living things at the cellular or molecular level for human purposes.

Scientists made the change so the corn would resist corn borers, insects that eat and destroy corn plants. The destruction can cost farmers one billion dollars each year.[2] These costs are passed on to consumers.

The new plants carried a gene from a soil bacterium, *Bacillus thuringiensis*. The gene causes the plants to make a poison, called Bt toxin (after the bacteria's name). The toxin is harmful only to insects, not to people or other animals. Bt toxin protected the plants from the European corn borer.

The genetic change was good for the corn plants. But was it bad for butterflies? Cornell University researchers reasoned that the corn plants' pollen would contain the Bt toxin. Wind could blow that pollen sixty meters (twenty-five yards) or more. What if nonpest insects ate it?

To find out, the researchers did some lab tests. They dusted milkweed leaves with pollen from Bt corn.

Some caterpillars that ate those leaves died. The specific caterpillars were the larvae of monarch butterflies. Each year, these beautiful orange butterflies migrate thousands of miles. The monarchs' path takes them right through the Midwest—America's "corn belt."

Monarch caterpillars do not eat corn. They eat the milkweed plant. Milkweed often grows near cornfields. Blowing corn pollen might still come in contact with the insects, the researchers reasoned.[3]

People love the sight of monarch butterflies. They did not love the idea that scientists were deliberately designing plants with a toxin. Public reaction was especially negative outside the United States. Groups in Europe and Japan refused to buy GM corn. Farmers faced a problem. Should they give in to public pressure and stop growing the pest-resistant corn? Some farmers did cut back. In 2000, U.S. farmers said they would plant 24 percent fewer acres of Bt corn than the year before.[4]

The cutbacks meant that non-Bt crops would be vulnerable to corn borers. Farmers could lose lots of income, and corn could become more expensive. Fighting the corn borers with chemical pesticides would also cost money.

Pesticide use raises environmental problems as well. Sometimes toxic chemicals poison animals and plants besides the targeted pests. Toxic chemicals can also make farm workers ill. Over time, pests develop resistance to chemical pesticides too. Then the farmers are back at square one.

Scientists such as John Beringer at England's

University of Bristol questioned the Cornell study. It did not account for wind dispersion or other factors.[5] Follow-up studies by other scientists suggested that the corn did not harm monarch caterpillars under real-world conditions.[6] A similar study on black swallowtail caterpillars showed no toxicity from Bt corn pollen under field conditions.[7]

Then, during the summer of 2000, John Obrycki of Iowa State University said he had confirmed that Bt corn harms monarch caterpillars. Obrycki's team placed milkweed plants near a Bt cornfield to collect windblown pollen. Then they fed the leaves to monarch larvae. About twenty percent of the caterpillars died. "Now we have a modified field study that shows an effect as well," said Obrycki.[8]

The Biotechnology Industry Organization objected. "Dr. Obrycki's research stands in the shadow of more than twenty independent studies by widely recognized scientific experts who have found that *Bacillus thuringiensis* (Bt) corn does not pose a significant risk to the monarch butterfly," said Val Giddings, the organization's vice president. Monarch butterfly populations had increased by roughly 30 percent during the previous year. During that same period, acreage planted with Bt corn increased too. If there were a problem, Giddings argued, monarchs would not be flourishing.[9]

In late 2000, the U.S. Environmental Protection Agency (EPA) held hearings. At that time, the agency said that Bt crops had "no unreasonable adverse effects" on human health or the environment.[10] A few months later, scientists advising the agency recommended further studies.[11] More studies conducted in 2001 said the corn did not hurt butterflies.[12]

Corn and caterpillars have focused the public spotlight on the biotechnology industry. A possible catastrophe for butterflies seems to have been avoided. Despite that, critics of genetically engineered food worry. What problems might lie ahead?

GM Food Throughout the Supermarket

Most Americans probably eat genetically engineered food every week. About two thirds of foods in American supermarkets may contain GM ingredients.[13]

Consider corn. In 1999, farmers planted Bt corn on over 28 million acres. That was about one third of the total U.S. corn crop.[14] Some of that corn goes to the supermarket's produce department. Some is canned and frozen so people can enjoy corn even when it is not in season.

Corn is an ingredient in many other foods too. The cereal aisle contains corn flakes, puffed corn, and other breakfast foods. The snack aisle carries corn chips, popcorn, and corn puffs. The baking aisle boasts cornmeal, cornstarch, corn oil, and corn syrup. These same ingredients are in foods ranging from cookies and candies to sauces, sodas, and salad dressings.

Soybeans are another big GM crop. In 1999, about half of the U.S. soybean crop was genetically modified.[15] Soybeans are an obvious ingredient in tofu (bean curd), soy milk, soy sauce, and veggie burgers. Soybean oil, lecithin (an emulsifier), soy protein, and other soy ingredients are in other products too. Ice cream, infant formula, snack chips, breads, cookies, and chocolates may all contain ingredients made from soybeans.

Canola oil comes from a crop called rapeweed or rape plant. Canola oil is in snack chips, fried foods, and salad dressings. Some of that is GM canola oil.

Many people do not think they eat cotton. But cottonseed oil comes from cotton. That cotton may be GM cotton. That oil can be used in cookies, crackers, and peanut butter.

Some farmers also grow GM tomatoes. They are an ingredient in ketchup, pasta sauces, salsa, pizza, and other foods. Some farmers grow GM potatoes, squash, papaya, and radicchio. These can show up in the produce department or in packaged foods.

Beyond this, materials used to process foods may have been genetically modified. For example, fermenting soaked grain with yeast is part of making beer. Genetically modifying the yeast can make the process more efficient. That helps beer companies produce various "lite" beers.

Farm animals that are not genetically engineered may eat GM foods. Some farmers also inject cows with hormones made through genetic engineering. They use the hormones so cows will give more milk.

Genetic engineering affects many foods. Those foods are in a wide range of products. Thus, most Americans probably already eat genetically engineered food.

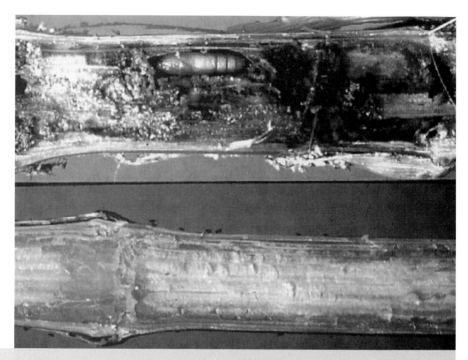

The stalk of corn on the top is ordinary corn that has been damaged by a corn borer, an insect pest. The bottom stalk is genetically engineered corn that has been protected from the corn borer by its Bt toxin.

Healthy or Harmful?

Genetic engineering in agriculture is a relatively young science. In 1973, biologists first spliced together DNA from different organisms. In 1980, the U.S. Supreme Court approved the first patent on a genetically engineered life form. Ananda Chakrabarty of General Electric had developed an oil-eating bacterium to help clean up oil spills.

Now GM crops are common. GM animals exist too. Some GM animals contain genes to make medicines. Examples are pigs, sheep, goats, and rabbits.

GM animals may soon enter the food supply. An example is a fast-growing salmon. An addition to the salmon's genes lets the fish make growth hormone all the time. Scientists initially got the added gene from a flounder. The GM salmon reaches market weight up to a year sooner than conventional salmon.

GM food is a booming business. In 1995, less than a million acres in the world grew GM food.[16] By 2000, about 100 million acres worldwide grew genetically engineered crops.[17]

Supporters say genetically engineered food is good. They say farmers can grow GM crops more efficiently. They claim GM crops save money, because farmers buy less pesticides and fertilizer. They say that also helps farm workers, because the workers are exposed to fewer chemicals. Fewer chemicals can help the environment. Perhaps most importantly, supporters say, GM food increases food production. It can help ensure a safe, healthy food supply for the world.

Opponents of genetically engineered food say it presents unacceptable risks. They fear environmental harm. They worry about possible health risks. They believe that too many questions remain unanswered. Critics also feel GM food is unnatural. Plus, big multinational corporations already seem to dominate agriculture. Critics say GM food extends that domination.

This book examines the science behind genetically engineered foods. Science constantly evolves.

As research continues, scientists will learn more. They will develop new types of genetically engineered species. They will ask more questions. They may discover new risks. They may explore new solutions.

This book also looks at arguments about genetically engineered food. Many groups have a stake: companies and universities that develop GM foods, farmers, companies that make packaged foods, the supermarket industry, government agencies, consumers, developing countries, and environmental groups. Each group has a different perspective. Also, not everyone in each group agrees all the time.

Many issues about GM foods cannot be expressed in black-and-white terms. A decision to stop growing Bt corn, for example, would mean people must deal with corn borers in another way. Increased pesticide use might adversely affect the environment and make people sick. It might even kill more butterflies. Other alternatives might mean a smaller harvest and less income for farmers.

On the other hand, continued use of Bt corn means critics will continue to worry about possible harm. Meanwhile, farmers and regulatory agencies must manage crops carefully. Otherwise, corn borers will quickly develop resistance to the Bt toxin and new pesticides would be needed.

Usually the debate about genetically engineered food takes place in the press and through meetings. Other times it spills into courts and public agency hearings. Sometimes it overflows into vandalism and violence by extreme environmental groups.

GM foods already have a far-reaching effect upon the world's food supply. They have the potential to become even more pervasive. Policy makers need to understand all sides of the debate in order to make wise decisions.

Consumers must make informed decisions too. Everyone wants a nutritious, affordable, healthy diet available year-round—not only for us, but for those in developing nations. What role, if any, should genetically engineered foods play?

2

How Genetic Engineering Works

The scientific study of genetics began in the 1860s. Pea plants fascinated Gregor Mendel, a monk who taught natural history.

Pure round pea plants bred with each other produced only round peas. Pure wrinkled pea plants bred with each other produced only wrinkled peas.

Crossing purebred round and wrinkled pea plants produced all round-pea offspring. When those plants matured, 25 percent of their offspring had wrinkled peas. The other 75 percent had round peas.

Mendel reasoned that each parent plant transmitted "factors of heredity" to offspring. Scientists now call those factors *genes*. Each organism that reproduces sexually receives one *allele*, or copy of a gene, from each parent.

If the offspring inherits identical alleles from each parent, it can only have that allele's trait. Pea plants with two alleles for wrinkledness have wrinkled peas.

If the offspring gets different alleles for a trait, the results depend on whether one allele is *dominant* or *recessive*. "Dominant" means that an allele's trait always gets expressed (or "shows up"). For peas, roundness is dominant over wrinkledness. If a plant has even one allele for roundness, its peas will be round. Roundness "wins" over wrinkledness.

The trait of wrinkled pea shape is recessive. An organism can carry a recessive gene but not have its trait show up. A recessive trait shows up only if the organism has two alleles for that trait.

Some alleles are not dominant over others, nor are they recessive. Then traits for both alleles can be expressed. For example, in one experiment, Mendel crossed white-flowered and red-flowered pea plants. All offspring had pink flowers. Mendel later bred the pink-flowered plants. A quarter of their offspring had red flowers. Another quarter had white flowers. The remaining 50 percent had pink flowers.

Mendel studied traits that involve single genes. Other traits involve multiple genes. Those traits have more complicated patterns of inheritance. So far, GM foods have involved traits related to single genes.

Delving into DNA

Nearly one hundred years after Mendel, James Watson and Francis Crick figured out the structure of molecules containing genes. Scientists call those molecules deoxyribonucleic acid, or DNA. Watson and Crick's work won them the Nobel Prize in 1962.

DNA molecules resemble long twisted ladders. The ladder "rails" are sugar and phosphate molecules. A pair of nucleic acids, or base pair, makes up each "rung."

Base pairs can contain four possible nucleic acids. They are adenine (A), thymine (T), cytosine (C), and guanine (G). Adenine's base pair partner is always thymine. Cytosine and guanine are always partners with each other. During normal cell division, DNA molecules unravel. Then each half forms the partners for its nucleic acids. The result is an exact copy of the original DNA.

Sequences of base pairs along the DNA molecule make up the individual genes. Millions of genes can fit on tightly coiled DNA molecules known as chromosomes.

In the 1860s, Gregor Mendel studied differences in the color and shape of peas in his experiments with plants.

Different species have specific numbers of chromosomes. Humans, for example, have twenty-three pairs of chromosomes, for a total of forty-six. Fruit flies have just four pairs, for a total of eight.

Single-celled organisms reproduce by simple cell division. Organisms like single-celled yeast and protozoa have DNA inside a cell nucleus. At cell division time, the DNA molecules unwrap themselves and move to separate parts of the nucleus. Each half makes its complement, and then the nucleus and the rest of the cell split. (This process is basically how normal cell division occurs as multicelled organisms grow.)

Bacteria are unusual single-celled organisms. Their cells lack a separate nucleus. Bacterial DNA often forms a long oval. Bacterial DNA also forms rings called plasmids. Plasmids sometimes move from one cell to another. This feature makes plasmids natural gene transport mechanisms.

Generally, the nucleus of every cell (other than egg or sperm cells) has all genes received from the parents. As multicelled organisms multiply, genes cause different parts of the organism to specialize. In other words, different genes are expressed, or "turned on," in particular cells.

Basically, the DNA in expressed genes controls protein production. The DNA tells parts of the cell containing ribonucleic acid, or RNA, to put amino acids together. The assembled amino acids form proteins.

Those proteins, in turn, control how the organism functions. Certain proteins determine how an organism grows. Certain proteins control the ability to digest certain foods. Other proteins regulate salt concentrations, metabolism, and so on. Most organisms need tens of thousands of proteins to function properly.

Breeding Before Genetic Engineering

Even before scientists "discovered" genetics, it was at work. Organisms of all types reproduced and transmitted genes to offspring. Likewise, even before people understood genetics, they used it for their benefit. So biotechnology is simply the latest development in this long trend of human use of agricultural knowledge.

Farmers have raised crops since ancient times. People have grown corn in Mexico for about six thousand years. Before that, people in the Middle East grew wheat and barley. People in New Guinea raised sugarcane. People in Indonesia raised yams and coconuts.

Each year, farmers saved some seed for the next year. Usually, the reserved seed came from plants with desirable traits. One desirable trait may have been high crop yield. Hardiness was probably another valued trait.

The genes passed on to future generations thus reflected the farmers' choices. In other words, people affected the crops' gene pools.

People have also raised and bred farm animals for thousands of years. By 8000 B.C., people in Iran and Afghanistan had domesticated goats and sheep.

By 6000 B.C., the ancient Chinese had tamed pigs and water buffalo. Meanwhile, people in Turkey raised cattle, and people in southern Asia raised chickens.

As with their crops, farmers bred animals to produce offspring with desirable traits. For example, a five thousand-year-old clay tablet from ancient Iran shows breeding records for donkeys. With animals as well as crops, then, people influenced the gene pool.

Since Mendel's discoveries, people have exercised much more control over plants' and animals' genetic makeup. Born in 1849, pioneering biologist Luther Burbank developed over eight hundred varieties of plants. Burbank's most famous "creations" include the Shasta daisy, the Burbank-Russet potato, and the white peach.

Burbank focused a lot on hybrids. Hybrids result when people crossbreed different varieties or species of plants. Burbank did not limit himself to varieties that grew locally. He imported plants from Japan, Australia, South America, and elsewhere. Many of Burbank's experiments crossed closely related species. Others crossed plants that were more distantly related. The plumcot, for example, came from crossing a plum with an apricot.

Crossbreeding is still a mainstay of conventional plant breeding. Computerized DNA screening helps scientists identify desirable genes more quickly. Other high-tech methods help scientists measure how well traits transfer, or move from one species to another.

When scientists cross two varieties of plants, the

offspring get half their genes from each parent. The desirable genes may transfer, but less desirable traits may transfer too. When a tomato gene for slower ripening transfers, for example, genes for tiny fruit may move too. Back-crossing is continued breeding that seeks to eliminate such "excess baggage," while keeping the desirable traits. Even with added growing seasons and computerized analysis, it can take years to successfully crossbreed a new crop variety.[1]

Some of Burbank's experiments also induced plant mutations. In a mutation, the cell's genetic makeup changes. The change can potentially be passed on to future generations. Some mutations occur on their own. Others happen in response to stresses.

Scientists still induce mutations today. Essentially, mutation is a way of expanding a species' available gene pool. Just growing cells in a petri dish (a round container for growing cells in a lab) can cause changes. Other times scientists expose cells to poisons or radiation in order to cause mutation. Linola, a linseed oil for human consumption, was developed in Australia with an induced mutation. The mutation eliminated most of the plant's linolenic acid. The acid makes traditional linseed oils harden into a film.

Modern plant breeding also includes unusual techniques. Haploid breeding forces plant sex cells to duplicate themselves. Then it makes the cells "mate" with their identical twins. The result is an organism with identical genes for every trait. Sometimes scientists also induce a plant to have more than two copies of all or some genes. Scientists have grown unusually large strawberries this way.

Animal breeding has changed too. If there is not a good bull nearby, artificial insemination of cattle is now an option. Thus, cows can bear calves sired by bulls that live many miles away.

Breeding between species sometimes occurs too. For example, mating a horse and donkey produces a mule. Usually, such offspring cannot reproduce.

What is new about genetic engineering? Traditional crossbreeding initially transfers many genes at once. Genetic engineering lets scientists target a specific gene they want to change.

Perhaps most importantly, scientists can now transfer genes between species that never could have mated in nature. Before, hybridization involved crosses only at the species or genus level. Now scientists can put animal genes into plants and do other combinations too. The key lies in recombinant DNA technology.

Gene Splicing 101

Recombinant DNA is "new" DNA that combines DNA from different sources. Biologists Stanley Cohen and Herbert Boyer first spliced together DNA from two different organisms in 1973. Over the last three decades, scientists have refined the technique and produced hundreds of GM organisms.

Scientists start by identifying traits of interest. One example might be a flounder's ability to survive in icy water. Another example might be a plant's resistance to a certain disease. Sometimes scientists get help from "gene banks." Gene banks contain data on genes that scientists have already studied.

Other times scientists must start from scratch. If no gene bank is available, scientists figure out what protein causes the desirable trait. Next, scientists calculate what DNA sequence would have directed a cell's RNA to make the protein. Armed with this information, scientists study the organism's chromosomes.

Sometimes the work goes quickly. Other times it takes years. Finally, scientists locate the gene of interest. In other words, they find the desired base pair sequence along a certain chromosome.

Next, scientists must separate that gene from the chromosome. Restriction enzymes, or restriction endonucleases, are chemicals that cut DNA. Scientists have discovered over eight hundred different restriction enzymes. Each works at a specific sequence of DNA base pairs. A restriction enzyme will snip DNA from any organism that has its target sequence. The organism could be a petunia, worm, fish, or even a cow. Also, restriction enzymes do not cut "straight across" base pairs of DNA. They leave one or more unpaired nucleic acids behind. Molecular biologists call such snipped edges "sticky ends." "Sticky" means that the unpaired nucleotides bond readily with their natural partners. For example, a lone adenine end will readily pair with another thymine.

Sticky ends let the snipped DNA join up with other lengths of DNA. Scientists put together the gene lengths they want. Then they strengthen the bonds with chemicals called ligases.

With recombinant DNA technology, scientists assemble DNA "packages" to insert into another organism. The packages usually include the target gene of interest, plus other genes that are discussed below. Generally the DNA packages are in the form of plasmid rings.

Scientists then get the plasmid ring into simple bacteria cells, such as *E. coli*. When fed and nurtured, the bacteria grow and multiply. They duplicate the DNA package. Thus, bacteria become "factories" to make many copies of the DNA.

Getting DNA into Another Species

Once scientists have many copies of their DNA package, they must deliver it into the plant or animal they want to modify. The method used depends on the particular species.

Sometimes a modified bacterium or virus "infects" a species with the DNA package. *Agribacterium tumafaciens* is one such DNA "taxi." In nature, the bacterium infects plants and makes them grow tumors. In the genetic engineering laboratory, scientists remove the bacterium's disease-causing traits. Then they insert their DNA package. The bacterium can carry the package into a plant and add it to the plant's own DNA.

With other plants, scientists "shoot" DNA packages into cultured plant cells. Scientists coat micron-sized particles of gold or other metal with the

DNA packages. (A micron is one-thousandth of a millimeter; five hundred microns would stretch across the diameter of a 0.5 mm mechanical pencil lead.) Scientists load the tiny pellets into the top of a chamber. Then pressurized gas "shoots" the particles into the plant cells.

With animals, scientists may use tiny needles to inject a DNA package into an embryo cell. The needle goes right into the nucleus.

After the transfer, cells go into lab dishes. Using various techniques, scientists stimulate them to grow. Plant cells can grow into whole new plants. Some animal embryos, such as mammals, must go into an adult's womb to develop fully.

DNA transfers can get very complicated. With plants, for example, cells that will receive altered DNA must be prepared just right. Otherwise, the cells will not grow into whole plants. Preparation methods vary from species to species too. With tomatoes, for example, scientists usually prepare cells from shoots. With soybeans, they begin with cells from premature seeds.

What Else Is in the DNA Package?

Just introducing DNA does not guarantee that it becomes part of target cells' own DNA. Suppose a gene gun shoots DNA into a clump of soybean cells. That clump could contain up to a billion cells.

"You'll have maybe a thousand cells that contain the gene, and maybe one in ten of those that will actually incorporate the gene into their DNA," explains John Finer at Ohio State University's Agricultural Research Center. Scientists cannot pick out those few cells just by looking at them. "It's a needle in a haystack," says Finer.[2]

It would be costly and time-consuming to grow the entire mass into mature plants and then search for the few with the transferred DNA. Instead, scientists put marker genes in the DNA package. Marker genes let scientists pick out which cells have the DNA package.

Some markers have been genes for resistance to antibiotics or herbicides. After DNA is introduced into a group of plant cells, scientists treat the cells with the antibiotic or herbicide. Most plant cells will die. Those plants that survive contain the resistance marker gene. Survival also means that the cells contain DNA for whatever trait the scientists want to transfer.

Some newer markers are genes for fluorescence. One such gene comes from a jellyfish. To see if the DNA package is present, scientists examine cells under a microscope with special lights and filters. If the sample glows, then it contains the DNA package.

The mere presence of a gene does not mean that it will function properly. The gene must be expressed. To encourage transferred genes to "turn on," scientists put promoter genes in the DNA package.

One promoter gene comes from the cauliflower mosaic virus. When it infects plants in nature, the virus gets its own DNA into plants' nuclei. Then the promoter encourages plant cells to "turn on" the virus's own genes. "It's like a light switch," explains biologist Adrianne Massey.[3]

The cauliflower mosaic virus's promoter gene works very effectively. "Think about what viruses do," says Massey. "Their whole goal is to get in there and hijack the plant's genetic machinery. That means they have to fool the plant cell's genetic machinery into making viruses."[4]

Of course, the whole virus would make the plants sick. Instead, scientists add just the promoter gene to the DNA package. The DNA package may also contain other genes designed to help the new plant or animal function.

Ready to Market?

While scientists select individual genes to put in the DNA package, they cannot yet control where those genes go in an organism. The package may "land" almost anywhere on an organism's chromosomes. Sometimes the DNA lands in a way that disrupts other functions of the organism.

Thus, containing the DNA package and expressing the gene of interest is not enough. The cells must also be able to grow into healthy plants or animals. Scientists may go through many trials before they get a healthy specimen with the traits they want.

That still is not enough. The GM organism must also transfer the trait reliably to future generations. This requires more trials and more research.

Finally, people who want to market a genetically engineered food must meet government requirements.

Even minimal regulation can involve reams of studies. It takes lots of time, expense, and patience to develop each GM species.

In Review

Scientists identify genes for desirable qualities. In the laboratory, they assemble DNA packages that have those genes, plus other genes. The other genes include markers to detect which organisms receive the DNA package. They also include promoters that turn on the target gene, plus other genes to help the transfer work.

Scientists then insert the DNA package into another species. Using markers, they determine whether the transfer is successful. Then scientists see how the GM organisms grow. If all goes well, the desired trait transfers to the other species without bad side effects.

This description is a simplified overview. Developing a GM organism usually takes years. It can also take millions of dollars. People paying to develop GM foods feel the investment is well worth it. Critics, however, question their motives.

3

Why GM Food?

One billion people suffer from hunger and malnutrition.[1] Without dramatic changes, the problem will get worse.

One hundred years ago, the earth supported only 1.6 billion people. By the year 2000, 6 billion people lived on earth. By 2030, the earth's population may swell to over 8 billion.[2] As population grows, the world's food demands will grow.

"Current technology allows us to feed about 5 billion," notes Alan McHughen at the University of Saskatchewan. "But we're running out of land, fossil fuels, water and other resources needed to

30

maintain current (pre-biotech) agriculture."[3] The Biotechnology Industry Organization says existing farmland must double production during the next three decades. Otherwise, there will not be enough food for the world's people.[4]

The United States, Canada, and some other countries have much fertile farmland. These countries grow enough food for their people. They even grow surpluses of foods such as corn and wheat.

Other countries are less fortunate. Some lack rich fertile soil. That limits what crops farmers can grow.

Climate plays a major role too. Torrential storms and floods devastate some countries' crops. Droughts dry up other areas' hopes for a good harvest. Soaring heat or freezing cold can also kill crops.

Genetic engineering may help the world's people cope with these problems. GM crops might grow and thrive despite harsh weather or poor soil. They may be able to resist diseases and pests. They may produce more fruits, vegetables, or grain. In short, genetically engineered food may increase the overall harvest from the world's farms. That can mean more food for hungry people.

For these reasons, supporters such as the Biotechnology Industry Organization call agricultural biotechnology "the future of the world's food supply."[5] They say GM food will feed the world's growing population. Norman Borlaug, winner of the 1970 Nobel Peace Prize, said it is "a delusion" to think the world's people can be fed without the latest technology.[6]

Some countries, such as the United States and Canada, have ample farmland. They grow enough food for their own people and are able to export such foods as corn, wheat, and barley (shown right) to other countries.

Critics say otherwise. The Union of Concerned Scientists says most work so far has focused on crops that produce profits. Scientists have done less research on foods that are common in developing countries, such as cassava, cowpea, or plantain. The Union of Concerned Scientists also questions whether GM food will really increase productivity better than traditional breeding. Water shortages, erosion, environmental abuse, trade policies, and other issues can cause food shortages too—with or without genetically engineered food.[7]

Other critics say the world already grows enough food. Food First/Institute for Food and Development Policy says the world's farmers produce 4.5 pounds of food per person daily.[8] Sadly, most poor people simply cannot buy enough food. Poor distribution systems make problems worse.

Unfortunately, the world's "haves" often do not share with the "have-nots." For example, as a result of improved agricultural technology, India faced a food grain surplus in 1999 and 2000. The government searched for a market to sell the grain. Yet millions of the country's people did not have enough food.

C. S. Prakash at Tuskegee University admits there are access problems. But he does not see them as a reason to deny technology to developing countries. Rather, he believes GM food can help poor people by increasing overall productivity.[9]

It would be wonderful to eliminate poverty, but it will not happen overnight. "It is unlikely that rich people will decide tomorrow to hand over all their money, and it's unlikely that farmers will continue to grow the food and then deliver it all, without payment, to the hungry around the world," Alan McHughen notes. "Biotechnology will not by itself solve the problems of hunger and poverty, but it will help immensely."[10]

Ultimately, countries with many mouths to feed must decide for themselves whether to use the technology. Some countries will face resistance. Poor farmers have joined with other groups to demonstrate against GM food in India, Bangladesh, the Philippines, Japan, Korea, and Indonesia.

Other people want genetically engineered food technology for their countries. Hassan Adamu served as Nigeria's minister of agricultural and rural development. Writing in the *Washington Post*, Adamu said that he resents activist groups that presume to know what is best for developing countries. To Adamu, GM food can "stop the suffering" of millions of hungry and malnourished Africans. Without it, he warns, many people will die.[11]

China has already welcomed GM crops. Government leaders want to improve the standard of living for China's 1.2 billion people. They do not want China to lag behind other countries in technology.[12]

Better Food Through Biotechnology

To be healthy, people need nutrients from different food groups—whole grains, fruits, vegetables, dairy, and proteins. Many people's diets do not provide this variety. Especially in developing countries, poor people often rely on a staple food.

A typical staple food is an inexpensive starchy food that is featured in most main meals. Rice is a common staple food in several Asian countries. Yams are a staple food in some African countries. Such staple foods provide energy and some important nutrients. They rarely fulfill people's entire nutritional needs.

Genetic engineering could make the world's food supply more nutritious. Scientists Ingo Potrykus and Peter Beyer genetically engineered Golden Rice. They added genes from a daffodil and a pea, plus a virus and bacterium. As a result, Golden Rice seeds contain beta carotene.

Beta carotene gives the rice grains' insides a golden yellow color. More importantly, beta carotene provides vitamin A. Over one million of the world's children do not get enough vitamin A in their diets.

They risk blindness, susceptibility to diarrhea, and other diseases. Fortifying rice with the vitamin could potentially prevent many cases of disease.[13]

Poor farmers in developing countries will not have to pay license fees to grow Golden Rice. Besides Potrykus and Beyer, the arrangement involved thirty-two companies and universities. They all felt the agreement was the best thing to do. "We are making sure that varieties important to the poor will be used," announced Potrykus, "not fashionable varieties for the urban middle class."[14]

Indian critic Vandana Shiva has called Golden Rice a "Trojan horse." It looks like a gift to the world's malnourished children. But Shiva says it is a first step in pushing GM food on poor people.[15] Likewise, Greenpeace has called Golden Rice "fool's gold." It says people would need over seven pounds of Golden Rice to get one day's requirement of vitamin A.[16] However, Golden Rice's promoters stand by the crop. For example, the Rockefeller Foundation's president, Gordon Conway, has said the rice can add enough vitamin A to diets to keep millions of children from dying or going blind.[17]

Despite criticism, other nutritionally enhanced foods are in the works. In Mexico, scientists at the International Maize and Wheat Improvement Center developed a high-protein corn. Early reports showed it had almost twice the usable protein found in other tropical corn varieties. It also could produce 10 percent more grain.[18] Ten percent more food could mean the difference between starvation and survival for a poor person in a developing country.

Scientists at the United States Department of Agriculture (USDA) developed a tomato with over twice as much lycopene as normal tomatoes. Lycopene may help prevent blindness in children. Lycopene may also reduce cancer risks and enhance cardiovascular health.

What else is possible? GM oil could contain less saturated fat. GM sugar might contain only half the calories. Even allergen-free peanuts are a possibility.

Better flavor and freshness are another goal. Okanagan Biotechnology of Canada developed a GM apple whose flesh would not brown so quickly when exposed to air. "You'll be able to cut this apple up and put it in the lunch bag and the kid might actually eat it," said company president Neal Carter.[19]

Carter and others hope the apple and other improved fruits may soon be available to consumers in the United States and Canada. "I strongly feel that this technology is here to stay," says Carter. "It takes senior level PhD scientists years (at least ten) to develop a new GE crop." Carter adds, "By

Cut this conventional apple open, and its flesh will soon turn brown from exposure to air. Would a GM apple that resists oxidation be a better treat?

the time they go to commercialization, they have been tested and characterized like no previous plant species in history."[20]

A Spoonful of Medicine?

Genetically engineered foods could also contain important medicines. Costs, transportation, and other factors can make vaccines expensive and hard to deliver in developing countries. Vaccines grown in a plant might cost less. They might also be more practical if refrigeration is not easily available.

Research sponsored by the National Institutes of Health has shown that GM potatoes can deliver vaccines to people. The GM potatoes stimulated volunteers' immune systems to make antibodies against an infection that causes diarrhea. Researchers have also developed GM potatoes with hepatitis B vaccine.

Might health officials in other countries really grow vaccines more easily than they now import them? While early studies involved potatoes, future research will likely use bananas, tomatoes, or other foods. Those foods would taste better raw and may be easier to use in the field. "The hope is that edible vaccines could be grown in many of the developing countries where they would actually be used," announced Regina Rabinovic of the National Institute of Allergy and Infectious Diseases.[21]

Developers stress that such foods would not be for everyday meals. "Our project is medicine food," said Yasmin Thanavala, a researcher at Roswell Park

Cancer Institute in Buffalo. "It's nothing you'll eat willy-nilly. It's more like a pill that you get from a doctor, a plant with a prescription in it."[22] Any medicine that looks like food would require careful security or need special packaging, to avoid accidental poisoning of people who thought it was just ordinary food.

Reaping What Is Sown

The more food a farmer can produce, the higher the profits will be and the lower the cost to consumers. Genetic engineering offers ways to control pests, reduce weeds, resist disease, and increase yield while reducing the use of chemical pesticides and herbicides.

America's agricultural industry has changed dramatically in the last century. The number of farms today is roughly a third of what it was one hundred years ago. Fortunately, those farms produce far more than they did then. Between 1940 and 1980, the United States more than doubled its production of seventeen leading crops.

Large machinery has automated many farm tasks. Breeding has improved the quality of seeds and livestock. Fertilizers help plants grow. Pesticides fight pests. Herbicides fight off weeds.

Food marketing has changed too. Foods routinely travel over one thousand miles before arriving at the supermarket. Many foods are still prepared from scratch. But many foods are now processed and packaged too. As a result, farmers get a smaller share of what consumers pay for food. The bulk of food costs goes to processors, packagers, transporters, markets, and others.

Increasing yield is one way farmers can make more profits without raising prices. GM crops that are hardier (stronger, or better able to survive poor growing conditions) than their counterparts can produce more. Likewise, GM crops that resist disease produce bigger harvests.

Reducing costs also increases profits. Corn borers, boll weevils, and other pests can literally eat away a farmer's profits. Pest-resistant crops can mean less costs for chemical pesticides. Some farmers growing GM cotton save over sixty dollars per acre.[23]

Herbicide-resistant crops can let farmers use a single type of weed killer. And the farmers may need less of that weed killer too. That can cut costs up to 40 percent.[24] In short, supporters say, GM crops offer farmers a chance to reap more profits from what they sow. Increasing profits to growers means that they can stay in the farming business and keep providing us with food to eat.

Environmental Benefits

Supporters of GM food say it helps the environment. Consider the problem of pests.

Measured by acreage, most American farms use chemical pesticides. Pesticides do kill pests, but they have problems. Many pesticides are poisonous.

Workers who spray the pesticides risk exposure to those poisons.

Many chemical pesticides do not just kill the target pest. They hurt beneficial, or helpful, insects too. Also, if a bird or other animal eats an insect exposed to pesticide, certain chemicals can harm them too. Bioaccumulation occurs when a harmful chemical is passed up the food chain and builds up in an animal's tissues. Some pesticides also persist in the environment. They take a long time to break down chemically. The chemical's toxic effects on the environment last even longer.

Pesticides raise health concerns too. Government regulations control how much residue can remain on food. But some people still worry about even small amounts of pesticides.

Last but not least, pesticides work only until pests evolve resistance. Basically, the pesticide kills off susceptible pests first. Insects with the greatest resistance survive. When they breed with each other, the offspring are also likely to resist the pesticide.

When insects evolve resistance, many farmers switch to another pesticide. The new pesticide may also present health or environmental concerns. It too has a limited useful life before pests evolve resistance to it.

"It's called the pesticide treadmill," explains entomologist Joseph Kovach at Ohio State University. "You burn up one; you get another one. You burn up one; you get another one." Kovach adds, "In theory our rules are toughening up on pesticide registration, so the newer compounds have a much better toxicological profile than the older compounds that we're losing."[25] To minimize problems, Kovach and other scientists advocate integrated pest management.

Integrated pest management combines several strategies to control pests. Rather than growing the same single crop every year, farmers could rotate crops. They might also intercrop, or grow different plants together in the same field. Sometimes one crop discourages the pests of the other crop.

Integrated pest management also encourages beneficial insects and birds. These animals are natural predators of pests. Ladybugs, for example, eat aphids, which are a pest of many plants, including tomatoes.

Bt crops, such as the Bt corn described in Chapter 1, produce their own pesticide. Other Bt crops include soybeans, cotton, and potatoes. Scientists have figured out DNA codes for over

This field of cotton has been infested by insects. The healthy cotton on the right contains a gene that causes it to make Bt toxin, which is poisonous to insects. The cotton on the left does not contain the gene, so it has been devastated.

fifty Bt toxins. Each type is supposed to target specific kinds of insects.

In the alkaline environment of insect guts, the toxin binds to cells. The cells cannot regulate water content properly. Soon the insects die from too much water. In contrast, most mammals—including humans—have acid in their stomachs. The acid breaks the toxin down into harmless chemicals, so that the animals are not harmed.

Bt crops build the pesticide into plants. That means less worker exposure to chemical sprays. It also means less chemicals sprayed into the air over a large area. Bt crops also make cleanup easier in case of a spill. Instead of worrying about whether chemicals got into water supplies, for example, workers would just sweep up seeds.

"When you're comparing this new technology to what we're currently doing," notes Kovach, "we generally seem to be moving forward."[26] Many chemical pesticides kill a wide range of insects—beneficial ones as well as pests. Studies debate whether Bt corn might affect other insects too. Yet the 20 percent mortality rates reported in some studies are still less than the kill rates for beneficial insects from some chemical pesticide sprays. "We seem to see more beneficials [helpful insects] in crops that are modified with Bt," Kovach observes.[27]

Weeds are another problem that plagues farmers. Weeding by hand costs too much in time and labor. Using machines to till, or plow, weeds under frequently risks erosion, or wearing away of the topsoil. Chemical herbicides, or weed killers, can control weeds. But many herbicides only work on certain kinds of weeds. To control all types, farmers often must use multiple chemicals. Some of those herbicides are very poisonous. One compound, for example, resembles the basic ingredient in nerve gas.

Glyphosate, glufosinate ammonium, and some other products kill many kinds of weeds. Some of these broad-spectrum weed killers are less toxic to the environment than other herbicides. Of course, they would kill conventional crops too. Herbicide-resistant GM crops provide an alternative.

In theory, GM crops with herbicide resistance should need less total herbicides than other crops. Also, the herbicides used can be less toxic than other ones farmers might use. Thus, supporters say herbicide-resistant crops are good for the environment and farm workers.

Roundup Ready soybeans, for example, are resistant to Monsanto Corporation's brand of glyphosate. A farmer can plant the soybeans and spray Roundup. The chemical should kill the weeds, but leave the soybeans standing.

Supporters of GM food say herbicide-resistant crops are better for people and the environment. Glyphosate, for example, is "less toxic than caffeine and aspirin," notes Adrianne Massey.[28] Plus, microbes in the soil quickly break glyphosate down into nonhazardous components. "It's gone in three days," says Massey.[29]

Critics challenge whether broad-based herbicides are as safe as they seem. Some people also suggest GM crops might result in superpests or superweeds.

Are GM crops really better for the environment? The jury is still out, say researchers LaReesa Wolfenbarger and Paul Phifer. Their review in the journal *Science* said there was not enough evidence yet to draw a definite conclusion either way.[30]

Meanwhile, farmers continue to plant seeds that make their own pesticides or resist weed killers. They feel they are protecting the environment and making work safer for employees.

Farmers who plant GM crops also feel their farms are more productive. Consumers probably will not see cost savings any time soon. One reason is that farmers get such a small share of what people pay at the supermarket. But better productivity means a higher income for the farmer. For many farmers, that makes a huge difference.

A Natural Extension

Supporters of genetically engineered food stress that it is a natural extension of traditional breeding. In their view, it is just faster and more precise. Traditional crossbreeding involves massive transfers of DNA. In contrast, genetic engineering transfers just a small package: the target gene, plus associated markers and promoters.

Yet is GM food just an extension of traditional agriculture? Does it seem weird for corn to have a bacteria gene? What about soybeans with a petunia gene? Should plants receive animal genes?

"Genes do not 'belong' to a given organism or species," notes McHughen. "Instead, many genes are common across many species. People who think it's creepy that corn carries a bacterial gene will freak out to learn that humans share some seven thousand genes with a microscopic worm (*C. elegans*)."[31] In addition, everyone eats bacteria all the time because they are present on our food, and we all have bacteria in our digestive systems.

Nor do supporters of GM food feel it is "unnatural" to move genes from one species to another. "This argument is based on the idea that Nature categorizes organisms into boxes we humans call species, and that genetic information from one box (or species) doesn't get exchanged with genetic information in another," says McIIughen. "Nature does allow gene exchange across species. Many plants can and do cross with other species, and even certain bacteria transfer genes into plants."[32]

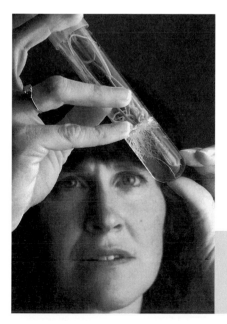

Genetic engineering plays an important role in environmental science. The process called bio-remediation uses GM organisms such as fungi, bacteria, and algae to clean hazardous waste

A geneticist looks at root growth on GM plants that may carry new genes for resistance to the disease Fusarium.

sites. The organisms "eat" contaminants and leave nontoxic by-products. Bioremediation is often cheaper and more effective than other cleanup methods.

Genetic engineering is also at work in the field of medicine. Some GM animals have genes that make them more likely to get cancer or other diseases. Scientists hope the animals will help them understand what causes disease. From there, they seek preventive measures or cures.

Genetic engineering makes medicines too. For years bacteria have produced most insulin for diabetics. Scientists genetically modified the bacteria to have the gene that produces the hormone. Genetic engineering also produces medicine for people with cystic fibrosis, AIDS, strokes, and other diseases. These medicines are readily accepted, say supporters. Why shouldn't people benefit from genetically engineered food too?

4

A Frightening Harvest?

"Genetic modification takes mankind into realms that belong to God and to God alone," declared Great Britain's Prince Charles.[1] Many critics of genetically engineered food agree with him. They feel that GM foods overstep the bounds of nature.

Before genetic engineering, most organisms evolved slowly. The world adapted to changes over time. Genes may have occasionally crossed species boundaries. But geography, physiology, and other factors limited what transfers were possible. And people did not pick and choose which genes to put where.

Now genetic engineering makes many novel gene combinations. Compared with past breeding, GM organisms enter the environment quickly. "It is all too big and is happening too fast," warned Harvard biology professor George Wald. "Restructuring nature was not part of the bargain."[2]

Geoffrey Clements of the United Kingdom's Natural Law Party voiced misgivings too. "The genetic modification of food is intrinsically dangerous," Clements warned. "It involves making irreversible changes in a random manner to a complex level of life about which little is known. . . . It must disrupt the natural intelligence of the plant or animal to which it is applied, and lead to health-damaging side effects."[3]

Greenpeace, the Organic Consumers Association, and other critics have a special name for genetically engineered foods. They call them "Frankenfoods." In Mary Shelley's novel *Frankenstein*, Dr. Frankenstein tried to create life. He succeeded—but he created a monster. Critics of genetic engineering fear it creates monsters too.

Genetic engineering changes a species' gene pool. People cannot fully control GM organisms once they enter the environment. In that sense, they are like a genie let out of the bottle. As Wald said, "Once created, they cannot be recalled."[4]

Supporters of GM food admit that changes to the gene pool occur. They disagree that this is cause for concern. After all, crossbreeding and other "traditional" breeding change the gene pool too. Supporters ask, why pick on one type of technology?

Health Concerns

Are genetically engineered foods safe to eat? Critics worry about possible dangers. They fear that GM foods will trigger allergic reactions.

Allergic properties can move between species. Pioneer Hi-Bred International wanted a soybean with more protein. It put a Brazil nut gene into a soybean. Then scientists at the University of Nebraska did tests. People with allergies to Brazil nuts ate the GM soybeans. They all had allergic reactions. Thus, the soybeans never went on the market.

Scientists test GM foods to see if their proteins are similar to known allergens. They also test proteins to see how fast they break down in stomach acid. Even with all the tests, scientists cannot guarantee that a new protein in the food supply will never cause an allergy. Scientists also cannot set a standard exposure level for how much of a protein might cause an allergic reaction.

Antibiotic resistance is another health concern. Unnecessary prescriptions, patients' failure to follow directions, and other factors have allowed some bacteria-resistant antibiotics to evolve. Could genetically engineered foods worsen the problem?

Remember that some GM foods have a marker gene for antibiotic resistance. What if the marker gene somehow transferred to people's intestinal bacteria? Then those bacteria might become resistant to antibiotics. Then antibiotics might not work when people get sick.

GM supporters say there is no evidence that this

An agricultural engineer makes juice from transgenic alfalfa. Critics argue that genetic engineering could cause dangerous changes in a plant's chemistry.

happens. Plus, some intestinal bacteria would already be resistant to antibiotics. Also, antibiotics used for marker genes tend to be older drugs. Many bacteria are already resistant to them anyway.

Surprise side effects of gene transfer are another worry. Altered genes could change a plant's chemistry. In one case, scientists genetically engineered yeast to increase fermentation. Compared with non-GM yeast, the engineered strain had higher levels of a potentially toxic chemical called methylglyoxal.

In another case, a company used GM bacteria to make L-tryptophan—a dietary supplement. It went on the market in 1989. Soon after, over three dozen people died from a disease called Easinophilia Myalgia Syndrome. The manufacturer recalled the product.

Critics like Genetic ID's John Fagan and English writer Luke Anderson suggested that genetic engineering caused the disaster.[5] Other observers say faulty manufacturing was probably the problem. The manufacturer had just switched to a new purification process. It could have left contaminants in the product.[6]

In still another case, rats fed GM potatoes suffered stunted growth. They had damaged immune systems too. GM food critics hailed the study as a warning. GM food supporters said the study lacked proper controls and had other flaws.[7]

Other critics say genetically enginecred foods' safety has not been tested fully. People who are already sick are willing to take some risks if a medicine may help them get better. But people who are well may resent GM ingredients entering their diet. "I find it amazing to think that the food industry in this country is carrying out experiments on us, the public, without our consent," complained one consumer to the Food and Drug Administration.[8]

Supporters of GM food say critics are wrong. "In fact, extensive scientific research has shown that foods derived through biotechnology are as safe as traditional foods," declared John Cady of the National Food Processors Association.[9] The Biotechnology Industry Organization claims GM foods have undergone more scientific testing than any other foods ever.[10]

In 2000, a National Academy of Sciences panel said genetically engineered foods appear safe. "The committee is not aware of any evidence that foods on the market are unsafe to eat as a result of genetic modification," concluded the report.[11]

An American Medical Association panel reached

a similar conclusion. "From all the research that's been done and all the information we have to date, genetically altered foods appear to be quite safe," reported Roy Altman.[12] Altman is a professor of medicine at the University of Miami. Altman presented the panel's report on behalf of the American Medical Association's Council on Scientific Affairs.

Critics continue to wonder. GM foods are barely a decade old. Might they cause long-term health problems someday down the road?

Superweeds?

What havoc might GM foods wreak in the environment? Pollen and seeds from GM plants do not always stay put. Wind can blow them to nearby areas.

Because of this, critics worry about superweeds. Suppose that GM plants crossbreed with wild "cousins." Canola, for example, is related to wild mustard. The offspring weed itself might resist weed killers. To kill it, farmers might need chemicals that may be harmful to the environment. Or they might not be able to kill it at all. The wild weed would be a superweed.

Critics agree that this has not happened yet. But they do not want to wait for disaster to strike. They feel no one has the right to impose any such risk on humanity.

Experience with invasive species provides an analogy. People planted the Japanese vine kudzu all over the South. The federal government even recommended kudzu for erosion control in the 1930s.

But kudzu has no natural enemies in the United States. The pretty weed spread out of control. Now people call kudzu "the vine that ate the South." Other "alien invader" plants in the United States include buckthorn, tamarisk, and leafy spurge.

Supporters of GM food dismiss the superweed fear. Herbicide resistance helps a plant survive only in a cultivated field. In a wild field, no one sprays herbicide. In theory, wild cross-pollinated plants should not have a competitive advantage.

A panel of scientists reported in 2001 that superweeds were already invading Canadian farms. They said that herbicide-resistant canola had crossbred with other canola plants. Some resistant offspring turned up as unwanted weeds in wheat fields.[13]

Another study in the journal *Nature* found no superweed problem. GM and non-GM crop plants both performed poorly when left to grow wild. In other words, even GM crops need a farmer's attention.[14] The researchers warned that they tested only certain GM crops. Modifications for different traits could produce other results.

The superweed issue is an open question. Critics worry about superweeds. Scientists must plan to avoid them.

Superpests?

Could GM crops worsen the very problems they are supposed to cure? Scientists have engineered various crops to produce Bt toxin. That toxin kills pests that can cause millions of dollars of crop damage. The goal is to reduce pesticide use.

Yet some hardy corn borers, boll weevils, or other target pests survive. If hardy survivors mate, their offspring could inherit resistance to the pesticide. Soon, only resistant pests will survive. Then the GM plants' pesticide would be worthless.

To combat such superpests, farmers would need more toxic pesticide sprays. Over time, pests could evolve resistance to those pesticides too. Farmers would then be back on a "pesticide treadmill." Over time, farmers would use stronger and stronger chemicals to control pests.

Organic farmers believe the problem would be even worse for them. Organic farmers choose not to use synthetic pesticides on their crops. Because Bt pesticide is produced naturally, some organic farmers spray the bacteria on their fields. If pests evolve widespread resistance to Bt pesticide, these organic farmers fear they will have no way to control pests. That could threaten their ability to make a living.

GM food supporters say proper management can handle pesticide tolerance. Guidelines for planting Bt crops generally require farmers to reserve some areas where they plant non-Bt crops. Scientists reason that these areas will provide a refuge, or safe place, for pests susceptible to Bt toxin. Susceptible pests could still mate. That, in turn, should slow evolution of resistance to the Bt pesticide.

The management strategy presumes that farmers will sacrifice some crop acres to pests. In other words, some loss is built into the system. Farmers accept that loss because otherwise they could lose their whole crop to the corn borer, bollworm, or another pest.

Different types of Bt crops, refuge areas, and rotation to regular pesticides are not the only options. The Organic Consumers Association, Greenpeace, and others prefer sustainable farming techniques. Sustainable methods are those that can be used indefinitely. In other words, they will not wear out. Examples include growing a variety of crops, encouraging natural predators of pests, and other methods.

Would a widespread switch to organic farming be feasible? Greenpeace, the Organic Consumers Association, and other groups say yes.

For Americans, organic farming may involve some higher food costs and reduced production. Crops with fewer pests, like soybeans, may be easier to grow organically. Other crops, like apples, may naturally have so many pests or disease problems that organic farmers may have more trouble.

Reduced production could be a serious worry in developing countries. For many Nigerian farmers, for example, fertilizer, herbicides, and pesticides are luxuries. "Organic" farming as practiced there does not produce enough food. Genetically engineered food, on the other hand, may let those farmers increase production.

The costs and benefits of organic farming can be debated both ways. Farmers want more production.

Pests and weeds compete for food and space. There are no easy answers.

Hurting Other Farmers

It is one thing for farmers to grow their own GM crops. But what if wind carries pollen from GM crop fields to a nearby non-GM crop field? Then a farmer might unknowingly raise GM crops. Later testing could reveal the contamination. Then that farmer might suffer financial loss.

South Dakota farmer Paul Sletten claimed that this happened to him. One of his neighbors planted StarLink corn during 2000. At the time, StarLink was approved for animal feed, but not for human food. When it was found in some foods, farmers had problems selling StarLink corn. Aventis CropScience, the company that licensed StarLink seed, helped the neighbor sell his crop. Meanwhile, Sletten claimed that StarLink had cross-pollinated his crop. As a result, Sletten said he incurred extra costs selling his corn. He complained to the U.S. Department of Agriculture.

"Not only does this create a problem of having to haul this contaminated corn to a special market," wrote Sletten, "I am also concerned that Aventis will be broke before I can receive any reimbursement for extra trucking, and also the twenty five cents per bushel premium for shipping to designated StarLink sites."[15]

StarLink is not the only crop that raises such concerns. Organic farmers do not use synthetic pesticides and weed killers. To have their crops labeled "USDA Organic," they must not grow GM crops. Normally, organic farmers charge slightly more to cover their higher costs.

If any GM crops cross-pollinate their crops, organic farmers could lose their certification. Farmers could still sell crops as food that was not certified organic. But farmers could not charge any premium then. Because of higher costs, the organic farmers would still lose money.

The Balance of Nature

Every ecosystem maintains a delicate balance in its food web. A food web outlines who eats whom in a habitat. For example, insects may eat various plants. Other insects or birds eat those insects. Larger animals eat them. Insects may feed on larger animals by biting them. Bacteria and fungi feed on all those organisms when they die. The web expands to include all the species in a particular area.

Alter one part of the food web, and effects may ripple throughout the ecosystem. Suppose farmers got rid of almost all weeds with GM crops and herbicides. Birds who ate the weeds' seeds might have much less food and move elsewhere.

GM food may interfere with the ecosystem in other ways too, warn critics. Suppose a fish farm raised GM salmon. Perhaps transferred genes helped the salmon grow larger. Then suppose some of those salmon escaped from the fish farm. In their natural habitat, the larger GM salmon may have a selective advantage over wild salmon. If so, they could endanger the wild salmon. Alternatively, the GM fish might crossbreed with native strains and weaken them.

GM food supporters say such scenarios are far-fetched, and that people could guard against any such small risk. Critics do not want to take that risk. Critics say that history proves that people cannot predict and prevent against all risks.

For example, chlorofluorocarbons, or CFCs, were welcomed as wonder chemicals. Thomas Midgely, Jr., introduced the first one at the American Chemical Society's 1937 meeting. Unlike other refrigerants, CFCs were neither toxic nor flammable. To demonstrate, Midgely inhaled a deep whiff of the chemical; then he safely blew out a candle. Now people could keep food safe from spoiling. At the same time, refrigerators would not poison people or start fires.

Unknown to anyone at the time, CFCs had a drawback. In the earth's upper atmosphere, CFCs broke apart molecules in the ozone layer. The ozone layer protects living things from harmful layers of ultraviolet radiation. Destruction of the layer could cause tragic environmental consequences on earth. In 1996, the world's industrialized countries agreed to stop producing CFCs. Some scientists still worry about CFCs' unforeseen effects on the environment.

In the 1980s, people unknowingly let the zebra mussel hitch a ride to the Great Lakes in ship ballast water. Without natural predators, the zebra mussels multiplied. They caused billions of dollars in damage to pipes, ships, and so on. Zebra mussels also crowded out many native freshwater mussels. The zebra mussel fiasco occurred by accident. Critics worry that something similar could happen with genetically engineered food.

Sterile species might reduce some concerns. Indeed, scientists can change some GM foods' genes so that any offspring grown from the seeds would be sterile. They could not produce a second generation of plants. The technology would prevent widespread proliferation. The technology would also increase company profits by assuring that customers buy new seed each year. But this idea—called "terminator technology"—has its own problems. Among other things, critics fear terminator technology would increase economic dependence upon large multinational corporations. Traditionally, say critics, farmers have always been able to save some seed to grow the next season. They say poor farmers cannot afford new seed each year.

For now, companies appear to have backed off from terminator technology. In large part, the move seemed to be a response to strong negative public reaction. Yet critics still feel concerned. Companies could, in theory, decide to pursue sterile-seed technologies in the future if public opinion seems more favorable.

Could GM foods reduce species' gene pools? Many farms practice monoculture—growing a single variety of a crop over a large area. If a GM crop were successful, many farmers might switch to it. They might grow just one or two varieties of each crop.

Why could this be a problem? Suppose that the

prevailing variety was susceptible to some disease. If that disease struck, widespread famine could result.

No such event has happened yet with GM food. Yet critics point to examples in history where monoculture left crops very vulnerable to disease. A mysterious disease attacked Ireland's potato crop in the 1840s. Over a million people died. The Irish potatoes had all come from genetically limited stock brought to Europe from South America.

Supporters of genetically engineered food say farmers are unlikely to grow only one or two GM crops. Also, researchers continually work on new GM crops. Supporters see little if any risk of "drying up" the gene pool.

Animal Suffering

Developing GM animals involves many of the same risks as developing GM plants. The transferred DNA package could attach to any chromosome. The gene of interest may or may not be expressed. The organism may or may not be healthy.

All this worries people concerned with animal rights. In one early experiment, USDA researchers added a human gene to pigs. The experiment failed in its goal of producing a faster growing pig. Instead, some of the test animals were very unhealthy. One sad specimen was arthritic, cross-eyed, and very hairy. Other animals could not even walk.

More recently, scientists transferred salmon growth genes into trout. The GM trout did not live as

Some opponents of genetic engineering are concerned that experimentation will result in the suffering of animals, who also may not be healthy and may not produce safe food.

long as non-GM trout. The GM trout also had abnormal skulls.

Critics of GM food say such animal experimentation is cruel. However, though GM food supporters do not want test animals to be unhealthy, they believe the tests' goals of developing better food or a new medicine source justify the experiments.

Universities and government institutions that fund animal research require scientists to follow specific ethical guidelines. Those guidelines aim to minimize any animal suffering. Despite that, many people still object to animal testing.

Critics also worry that genetic engineering could make animals more susceptible to certain diseases. GM bacteria produce bovine growth hormone. Some farmers inject it into their cows. The hormone increases the cows' milk production.

The cows themselves are not GM animals. But critics say the hormone can cause disorders of the uterus or ovaries. People who sell the hormone say proper management can avoid problems.[16]

But some farmers say their herds still get sick. Other people question whether milk from treated cows is safe. They worry that the hormone might somehow affect people, perhaps by speeding the onset of puberty or by fostering obesity. They worry despite assurances from the American Medical Association and the federal government that the cow's milk is safe.[17] Should they worry, or should they trust the government?

A GM animal would also have an altered body chemistry. In theory, scientists should make sure any GM animals were healthy before letting farmers breed them. Yet critics say scientists cannot detect all long-term consequences. Should critics still worry about potential cruelty to animals?

A related question is whether GM food wrongly interferes with organisms' "speciesness" or identity. Critics say that changing a species to suit human needs seems inconsistent with efforts to protect endangered species. Supporters say this is done in any type of breeding. Plus, they say, a few changed proteins do not alter a whole species.

Multinational Monsters?

Supporters of genetically engineered food say it offers hope to feed the world. Critics say large multinational corporations just want to make more money. Profit, not science, drives the move to GM foods, say critics.

Patent rights add to critics' concerns. Patents reward inventors with a limited-time monopoly on their inventions. In theory, the monopoly encourages companies to invest time and money in research. It also encourages companies to make technology available through licenses.

What happens when patents expire? Monsanto produced Roundup, a form of glyphosate, a broad-spectrum weed killer. Shortly before its patent on glyphosate expired, Monsanto began marketing Roundup Ready crops. These GM crops can survive the broad-spectrum weed killer glyphosate. But sellers of Roundup Ready seeds have required farmers to use Roundup, Monsanto's brand of glyphosate. By contract, the farmer cannot use a competitor's brand, even if it is chemically similar.

From the seed seller's perspective, the contract terms provide quality control. Monsanto cannot control how other companies make herbicides. It only guarantees the GM crops' effectiveness against the Roundup brand.

From critics' perspective, the license terms simply extend the monopoly. In 2000, Monsanto had $2.6 billion in Roundup sales.[18] The law may let other companies make glyphosate herbicides. But farmers will not buy from other companies if their contracts require them to use Roundup.

Some patent right grants have been overbroad. In one 1994 case, the European Patent Office granted Agracetus rights for all GM soybeans—not just the kind developed by that company. In effect, Agracetus got a huge monopoly. The patent prevented anyone from using or selling any kind of GM soybean in Europe for seventeen years, without the patent holder's permission. Subsequent grants of rights have been narrower. Critics like Rural Advancement

This field of Roundup Ready corn is resistant to Roundup, a herbicide. Monsanto, the company that makes it, says Roundup is less harmful to the environment than other herbicides. Opponents of genetic engineering say that Monsanto will have a monopoly on both the herbicide and the seeds.

Foundation International (RAFI) still object. They do not want agricultural technology rights concentrated among a few large companies.[19]

Another worry is that GM crops might replace the broad variety of crops presently grown in developing nations. Poor farmers could become more dependent on large corporations' monopoly power. The gap between the world's "haves" and "have-nots" could increase.

GM food supporters stress that seed variety is not the problem. Third-world farmers who practice subsistence farming already do poorly. Anything that can help is worth it, say GM food supporters. Critics counter that dependence on multinational corporations is not the way. Critics want social reform—not the risks that they say come with genetically engineered food.

Fear of the Unknown

In Greek mythology, the gods told Pandora not to open a certain box. Pandora's curiosity overwhelmed her. She had to know what the box contained. So, she opened it anyway. When she did, Pandora let loose a slew of problems into the world.

Critics like George Gaskell at the London School of Economics have called genetic engineering a "Pandora's box."[20] They say scientists are so busy exploring what they can do that they fail to consider potential risks. They fear that GM food will unleash its own slew of unknown problems.

People have identified some potential problems.

Critics say those issues are serious enough to stop GM foods. Supporters either dispute those issues or say they can be managed wisely.

But people do not foresee all problems. DDT is a case in point. At first DDT protected World War II troops. It killed mosquitoes and other insects that could transmit malaria, typhus, and other diseases. Later, public health officials continued to use DDT to control disease. Elizabeth Whelan of the American Council on Science and Health estimates that DDT has saved a hundred million lives.[21]

After World War II, farmers welcomed DDT. It remained active for a long time, so farmers did not need to respray as often as with other chemicals. The chemicals killed pests efficiently. Farmers reaped larger harvests.

Then in 1962, Rachel Carson published *Silent Spring*. Carson's research showed that DDT hurt other species too. Opponents criticized Carson harshly, but later research supported her.

Basically, birds and other animals in the food chain ate insects affected by the spray. DDT built up in those animals' systems. Peregrine falcons, for example, laid eggs with very thin shells. Young birds could not hatch, and the peregrine population plummeted.

Finally, the United States government banned DDT. Some developing countries still use DDT to control mosquitoes. They are more worried for now about the immediate threat of malaria and other diseases. But the chemical can clearly have far-reaching environmental consequences. People did not foresee those problems sixty years ago.

Critics fear that similar unknown problems will result from genetically engineered food. Scientists cannot predict every consequence of a gene transfer. As a result, critics argue, how can anyone adequately guard against all potential risks? And why should people trust large corporations who profit from GM food to protect them?

On the other hand, argue GM food supporters, who else has resources and the incentive to develop new technology? They say education can help people overcome the fear of the unknown.

Critics of genetically engineered food do not accept such assurances. They remain suspicious of companies that stand to profit from genetically engineered food.

5

Government's Role

Three federal agencies regulate GM food in the United States. They are the United States Department of Agriculture (USDA), the United States Environmental Protection Agency (EPA), and the Food and Drug Administration (FDA).

Agencies try to stay neutral when doing their job. Former Secretary of Agriculture Dan Glickman explained, "Government regulators must continue to stay an arm's length, dispassionate distance from the companies developing and promoting these products; and continue to protect public health, safety, and the

68

environment."[1] In other words, agencies must not appear to take sides if they want to retain public confidence.

Secretary of Agriculture Ann Veneman, Glickman's successor, views GM food optimistically. "The technologies of the new century—biotechnology and information technology—will reinvigorate productivity growth in food and agriculture production and . . . make agriculture more environmentally sustainable," she said in late 2001.[2]

The USDA has general authority over the farming industry. The USDA's Agricultural Research Service studies genetic engineering. Its researchers also develop new foods.

The USDA's Animal and Plant Health Inspection Service regulates the importation and field testing of GM foods. The Economic Research Service and Agricultural Marketing Service deal with marketing and its economic impacts. USDA inspectors develop and enforce standards for food handling.

At least until 2001, most farmers and processors mixed GM and non-GM crops together. Thus, GM corn and non-GM corn went into the same silo. GM soybeans and non-GM soybeans got stored together too.

That system could well change. Some foreign markets and grain processors do not want genetically engineered foods. A system that separates GM and non-GM foods may help farmers sell crops more easily. In November 2000, USDA invited members of the public to comment on whether USDA should accredit, review, or certify systems for preserving the identity of GM and non-GM foods.[3] In 2001, Monsanto agreed to help set up a system to segregate GM wheat.

The EPA's job is to protect the environment. Among other things, the EPA regulates pesticides. It decides which pesticides people can use. It determines how much residue can remain on foods.

The EPA views GM crops that make insect toxins as pesticides. Thus, the EPA regulates Bt crops like corn, soybeans, and cotton. EPA rules detail how pesticides that are incorporated into plants must be evaluated to ensure protection of human health and safety. As of 2001, the rules included most plant-incorporated pesticides in GM plants. Except for limited cases, the rules exempted plants that were developed through conventional breeding.

The FDA's jobs include food safety. Basically, the FDA compares GM foods with their non-GM counterparts. In general, the FDA has said that genetically engineered foods are "substantially equivalent" to their non-GM counterparts. Companies must provide warning if the food can trigger unexpected allergic reactions. Companies must also say if nutritional value differs from the non-GM food.

"FDA is confident that the bioengineered plant foods on the U.S. market today are as safe as their conventionally bred counterparts," Joseph Levitt of the FDA's Center for Food Safety and Applied Nutrition told a Senate committee. "To date, there is no evidence that these plants are significantly

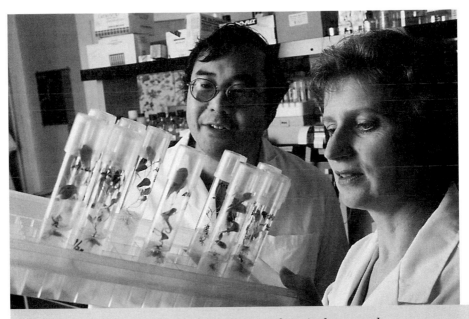

Scientists at the U.S. Department of Agriculture study some genetically engineered guayule plantlets. The USDA develops new foods and is responsible for regulating the farming industry.

different in terms of food safety from crops produced through traditional breeding techniques."[4]

The FDA consults with developers before new GM foods go on the market. For several years, this process was informal. That is, people did it, even though rules did not require review. As part of the informal process, developers submitted huge stacks of data for review.

Then the FDA decided there should be formal premarket notice. In other words, developers would have to submit specific materials required by rules before selling a new crop. The materials should include both favorable and unfavorable information that the developer knows about the product's safety, nutrition, or other regulatory issues. The FDA also anticipated that developers will continue to consult with the agency and respond to any concerns the FDA might raise about the new products. "These initiatives will further assure that all food products developed using the tools of modern biotechnology are known to the Food and Drug Administration, so that FDA can continue to examine these products before they reach the market," announced FDA commissioner Jane Henney in January 2001.[5]

Industry groups like the FDA's position. "Most importantly, there is again renewed acknowledgement that food biotechnology is safe," said Lisa Katic of the Grocery Manufacturers of America.[6]

Carl Feldbaum of the Biotechnology Industry Organization said the FDA's process provides "renewed confidence" in the United States' food supply. "The U.S. regulatory system is a model around the world because it is grounded in science, not superstition or uninformed emotion," said Feldbaum.[7]

Critics of genetically engineered food disagreed. "Industry likes this because it's business as usual," complained Charles Margulis, a genetic engineering specialist with Greenpeace. Although notice is required, he said, safety testing is not. "It's up to the companies to decide what to submit [and] what not to submit, what kind of tests to do [and] what kinds of tests not to do."[8]

Similarly, Carol Tucker Foreman of the Consumer Federation of America said the only evidence of safety would be "the opinion of the manufacturer."[9] Andrew Kimbrell of the Center for Food Safety noted, "Under these rules, American consumers will still be the guinea pigs testing the safety of these foods."[10]

For these and other reasons, critics of genetically engineered food want stricter rules. If the agencies will not change the rules themselves, critics may seek help from Congress.

Label Wars

Currently, United States law generally does not require any special labels for GM foods. Rather, the FDA requires a label if an ingredient could cause a significant allergic reaction. The FDA also requires a label if nutritional information differs significantly from the conventional food. Otherwise, companies can sell most GM foods just the same as non-GM foods.

At the very least, opponents of genetically engineered food demand labels. Without labels, consumers do not know if a particular product contains GM ingredients. As a result, critics say, consumers have little choice about what they eat.

"Opinions on biotech foods' safety will always vary," one consumer wrote to USDA, "but regardless, all interested parties must be afforded the right to know, and consequently given the right to choose, what they are about to purchase."[11] "We have an absolute right to know what is in the food we are purchasing, as well as how it was produced," another consumer wrote to the FDA.[12]

Critics distrust companies that do not label GM foods. "I am particularly concerned that the USDA and the companies which promote this technology do not have enough faith in the safety of the technology to market it openly and to clearly identify products containing modified ingredients," commented organic farmer Tanya Russ.[13] Given a choice, opponents say people would prefer non-GM foods. Labeling, they say, would end companies' unfair profits from GM crops.

Even groups that do not specifically oppose genetic engineering have endorsed labeling. "Consumers should have the right of informed choice regarding the selection of what they want to consume," announced a December 2000 report by the U.S.-EU Biotechnology Consultative Forum.[14] The forum included representatives of consumer, industrial, and academic groups from the United States and the European Union.

A *Christian Science Monitor* editorial went so far as to say the issue was a "no-brainer." If people want to know, it said, then companies should provide the information.[15]

Even a former biotech company executive expressed support. "How could you argue against labeling?" said Roger Salquist, former chief executive of Calgene, a biotech company. "The public trust has not been nurtured."[16]

Other people say the issue is not that simple. Labeling genetically engineered foods would require segregation of GM crops. That would require a separate distribution and handling system: separate silos, separate machinery, separate railcars, etc. Factories making processed foods would need to commit to either GM or non-GM ingredients, or they would need separate production lines. In short, separation would require higher costs all around.

On the other hand, separation may become more common soon anyway, as discussed above. If that happens, labeling would be easier.

Adrianne Massey, who favors genetically engineered foods, has other objections to mandatory labels. Massey feels that all foods have been genetically modified. That is, all foods reflect some breeding choices by humans. Why single out recombinant DNA technology from other methods of developing foods? "To me, it's as irrelevant as saying this could contain something that came from a plant," she says.[17]

Massey also thinks that a label requirement would imply that genetic engineering should make a difference in consumers' nutritional decisions. But, she says, no evidence proves that GM foods are any less safe or nutritious than other foods. Thus, she thinks any required label would be misleading.

"The concept of labeling for just the sake of it is not helpful," says Massey. "Because once you establish that precedent and say the FDA no longer cares if labels are accurate or misleading, think of what could end up on labels, and think of how confused we'd all be."[18]

Despite that, some people care very deeply about whether they eat GM foods. "It occurred to me that the most efficient way to label would be for firms

Do you know which products in your grocery cart contain GM ingredients? Currently, federal law does not require companies to label products one way or the other.

to label foods that didn't contain genetically modified ingredients," says Ohio State University economics professor Ian Sheldon.[19] Some businesses would then serve the special market of consumers who did not want GM foods. That would involve costs, but companies could pass those costs along to consumers. For years, the organic food industry worked that way.

Yet labeling may not simply be a matter of economics, admits Sheldon. "Economists have a hard time dealing with this notion that maybe consumers feel they have a right to know about whether foods do or don't contain GMOs [genetically modified organisms]," notes Sheldon.[20]

In late 2000, USDA unveiled new standards for when a food can be labeled as "organic." The label will mean that a food was produced without pesticides, growth hormones, or irradiation. The "USDA Organic" seal will also mean that a food was produced without genetic engineering. "I am proud to say that these are the strictest, most comprehensive organic standards in the world," announced Dan Glickman, who was then secretary of agriculture.[21]

The "USDA Organic" label should function as the "pay-if-you-care" model. Thus, it gives consumers who want to avoid GM food a way to do that.

But most food sold in stores is not organically grown. Thus, most consumers may not know whether or not their food contains GM ingredients. A label could say that it *might* contain some GM ingredients. That may be too vague to satisfy people who want to know one way or the other. A label could also designate ingredients as GM if they made up more than a certain percentage of the product. That system still may not satisfy people who do not want any genetically engineered foods at all.

Would a label saying a food had GM ingredients turn consumers away? A tomato paste whose label said it had GM tomatoes sold better than competing brands at England's Sainsbury's supermarkets. Perhaps customers liked the label's environmental reasons for using GM ingredients.[22] Or perhaps the GM brand was less expensive than its competitors.[23] Of course, no one knows who would have bought the product if it did not have GM ingredients.

In 2001, the FDA began a system for voluntary labeling of foods. The agency's guidance would not require companies to label foods one way or the other. But it would let companies provide information to consumers if they wanted.

"While the use of bioengineering is not a material fact," said the FDA's draft, "many consumers are interested in the information, and some manufacturers may want to respond to this consumer desire."[24] If companies do use a label, FDA wants to make sure that no statements are misleading.

"The new labeling guidance is also a win for consumers," said Lisa Katic of the Grocery Manufacturers of America. "It allows the maximum amount of individual choice while ensuring that food manufacturers' claims are truthful."[25]

Greenpeace's Charles Margulis disagrees. "Saying the companies can label their products non-GMO is putting the burden on the wrong foot." Companies using GM ingredients are the ones engaging in a "genetic experiment." They should have to pay for labeling, says Margulis. Instead, government says that companies who use the same non-GM ingredients they always have can pay for labels. "It's really a regulatory Alice in Wonderland," says Margulis. "It's a completely backwards way of doing it."[26]

Congress has gotten involved too. Ohio Democrat Dennis Kucinich, for example, sponsored legislation to require labels on GM foods. Currently, no such bill has yet become law.

If companies had labeled all GM foods from the start, critics may not have objected as much. Now the issue goes beyond what the law requires. Ultimately the issue will depend upon what consumers demand.

Tacogate

The GM food debate turned to taco shells in September 2000. Genetic ID of Iowa found evidence of StarLink corn in taco shells. Kraft Foods sold the particular taco shells under the Taco Bell brand name.

StarLink had approval for animal feed. But that GM corn was not allowed in human food. Genetically Engineered Food Alert, a group that opposes genetically engineered food, wanted the FDA to recall the taco shells.[27] When additional tests confirmed the results, Kraft Foods recalled millions of taco shells.

"Tacogate" was not over yet. Testing found StarLink in corn flour, grits, chips, soup, and other products. It even showed up in tiny corn flakes used to make beer.

Debate shifted to StarLink corn's potential risks. StarLink has a Bt gene to protect it from the corn borer. Other Bt corns already had approval for human food. The StarLink gene came from a different strain of Bt bacteria. It made the corn plant produce a protein, Cry9C. Cry9C attacked a different part of insects' guts. Aventis CropScience hoped its product would help farmers postpone insects' resistance to Bt toxin.

Unlike protein from other Bt corn, Cry9C showed greater resistance to heat and digestive juices. In other words, the protein was more likely to survive the human digestion process. That raised questions about the potential for allergic reactions.

Mere exposure to other cells does not prove there is a health problem. Cry9C did not resemble other known allergens. Little, if any, Cry9C was present in any of the tested food products. "You're starting out with a very low amount of protein in the corn to begin with," noted Michael Phillips of the Biotechnology Industry Organization, "and then it degrades considerably to the point where you can barely detect it."[28]

As a result, some people argued that StarLink corn was safe. "A strong case can be made that this is no hazard," said Phillips.[29] "I do not believe it's likely to cause any allergies," noted Rockefeller University professor T. P. King.[30] "In my opinion," said University of Nebraska's Steve Taylor, "there is virtually no risk associated with the ingestion of StarLink corn in this situation."[31] The EPA also said it "believes the risks, if any, are extremely low."[32]

The absence of a known allergen does not mean someone cannot get sick. Allergic reactions often require exposure for an extended time. With a new protein, people may not yet have developed sensitivity. In other words, they may not yet know if they have an allergy. "We don't know and the EPA

This teen is comparing labels on different tofu packages. USDA rules adopted in 2000 spell out procedures for products to be certified as organic. Among other things, products that carry the certification would not be produced with genetic engineering.

doesn't know and the allergists don't know," argued Jane Rissler of the Union of Concerned Scientists.[33]

Also, allergens are different from poisons. Poisons usually require a minimum amount to make someone sick. But even the tiniest bit of an allergen may trigger a reaction in sensitive people. After the taco recall, some people said they had gotten sick. The government could not confirm those reports.[34]

In any case, the EPA canceled StarLink's registration in October 2000. Thus, farmers could no longer grow it. "Because Aventis was responsible for ensuring that StarLink corn only be used in animal feed, and that responsibility clearly was not met, today's action was necessary," the EPA's Stephen Johnson explained. Any remaining StarLink corn could be used for animal feed or industrial uses.[35]

Tacogate affected the market for corn. A class-action lawsuit was filed on behalf of farmers in December 2000. It claimed no one had warned farmers about StarLink's selling restrictions. Because farmers did not separate StarLink from other corn, the complaint said they lost money. The complaint also said that StarLink contaminated neighboring farmers' crops through cross-pollination. "Now the whole credibility of the American corn market is taking a beating and people who did not plant StarLink corn cannot sell their crop in several markets," claimed plaintiffs' lawyer Richard Lewis.[36]

In January 2001, Aventis CropScience made an agreement with seventeen states. The company would pay farmers for losses they suffered because StarLink corn entered the food supply. Costs could

range anywhere from $100 million to $1 billion.[37]
Soon after, Aventis fired three top executives.

Tacogate fueled fears about the general safety of
GM food. "Foreign governments and consumers who
had been having doubts about the safety and
integrity of U.S. exports were given good reason to be
concerned that food coming from the U.S. was not
meeting guarantees of safety," noted Environmental
Defense Fund scientist Rebecca Goldberg.[38]

Tacogate raised questions about government regulation too. In a report prepared for the Consumer
Federation of America, Thomas McGarity and
Patricia Hansen of the University of Texas Law
School criticized the government. "This is a regulatory system that doesn't regulate, because of
exemptions that create gaping holes," said McGarity.
"Consumers are told public agencies are looking at
these products when in fact they are not."[39]

Indeed, why would an agency limit StarLink's
approval if the existing grain distribution system
could not assure compliance? In 2001, the EPA said
it would no longer give such conditional approvals.[40]

As a separate matter, why would a company sell
seed without making sure all customers knew about
any restrictions? How much clout do the agencies
really have? These and other questions linger.

6

To Market, to Market

How do GM foods fare in the supermarket? Consider the case of Flavr Savr tomatoes. In 1994, Flavr Savrs became the first genetically engineered food sold directly to consumers. Calgene, Inc., had changed the tomatoes' genetic makeup to slow the ripening process. The tomatoes would arrive fresh at supermarkets. They would have a longer shelf life.

Until then, most supermarket tomatoes were picked green. Some had just the slightest tint of red. The tomatoes "ripened" artificially with ethylene gas.

They got to stores before rotting. But most of them tasted bland. Wouldn't people prefer tasty tomatoes that naturally stayed fresh longer?

Calgene spent over $20 million developing and getting approval for Flavr Savrs. Finally, the FDA gave its okay. Market analysts predicted big profits.

Calgene began selling Flavr Savrs as McGregor brand tomatoes. The huge profits never rolled in. Instead, Calgene lost money.

Why did Flavr Savrs fail? Different people cite different reasons.

Perhaps consumers did not want GM food. At one Illinois supermarket, the Pure Food Campaign staged a "tomato dump." Protesters urged consumers not to buy the tomatoes.

Perhaps the Flavr Savr could not live up to its promises. The Union of Concerned Scientists said the crop sometimes gave low yields or suffered disease. Other times, the tomatoes were mushy or bruised.[1]

Some people said Flavr Savrs tasted awful. Who wants a good-looking tomato if it tastes like cardboard? Plus, scientists had also been crossbreeding tomatoes to slow the ripening process. Some people preferred those "traditional" tomatoes' taste.

Other consumers liked Flavr Savrs. "People enjoy the flavor," said grocer Bert Gee in Davis, California. But supply was sometimes a problem. On those occasions, said Gee, "We actually had to put a limit on what people could buy: two per family or four per family."[2]

Indeed, Flavr Savrs were only sold in limited

markets. Calgene had lots of science know-how. It did not have a good nationwide distribution system.

Perhaps its high price doomed the Flavr Savr. To recoup its investment, Calgene charged a premium. Many consumers did not want to pay two dollars per pound. Competing brands cost less.[3]

The Flavr Savr story is like an old fable about blind men and an elephant. Each man touched a different part of the elephant. As a result, all described the animal differently. For instance, the man who touched the tail said, "An elephant is like a rope," while the man who touched the leg said, "An elephant is like a tree."

Likewise, analyses about GM food depend on people's perspectives. Although other factors hurt Flavr Savrs, bad business judgments probably hurt Flavr Savrs the most.

Companies Respond to Consumer Fears

Genetically engineered foods are more common now than when Flavr Savrs went on the market. Yet activist groups and some consumers complain. Food companies do not want to lose sales, so they respond.

In 1999, Unilever UK and Nestle UK announced that they would phase out GM foods. Both companies sell substantial amounts of food in various countries. They each took the step after European consumers voiced strong opposition to genetically engineered foods.

In 2000, Frito-Lay told its supplier farmers not

to plant either GM corn or GM potatoes. Frito-Lay makes various snacks, including tortilla chips, corn chips, and potato chips. "We are hearing from our consumers that there is confusion," noted Frito-Lay spokesman Lynn Markley.[4]

Soon after, Novartis A.G. announced that its food products no longer had GM ingredients. The company's products include Gerber baby foods, Ovaltine, and Wasa crackers.[5] Even Iams pet food said it would not use GM ingredients.[6]

Why the shift? Food companies do not want to say that GM foods pose any health or environmental problems. But they want to be sensitive to consumer concerns. Companies also want consumers to view their foods as quality products. An image of wholesomeness is especially important for products like baby food.

Moves away from GM ingredients aim to please consumers, but still they draw criticism. The American Council on Science and Health (ACSH) says that GM food is supported by sound science. When Frito-Lay switched to non-GM corn and potatoes, ACSH's president Elizabeth Whelan criticized the company. "American consumers are better served by corporate leaders who stick with science," wrote Whelan, "instead of running for the tall grass the moment strident, ill-informed critics of food technology try to foment unfounded fears."[7]

To complicate matters more, companies' actions can be inconsistent. After Novartis's action, Gerber baby foods no longer had GM ingredients. But Novartis's agricultural division still sold GM seeds.

McDonald's asked its suppliers not to send GM potatoes for its French fries. Meanwhile, company franchises used vegetable oil to cook those fries. It is unclear whether any of that oil came come from GM corn, canola, or soybeans.

Still other companies resisted consumer and activist group pressure. In 2000, Campbell's Soup Company's John Faulkner said the company believed that GM ingredients were "equally nutritious and equally safe" as non-GM ingredients. Besides, suppliers of corn, soybeans, and other crops routinely mixed GM and non-GM varieties. "We don't control the supply chain," noted Faulkner.[8]

Sara Lee executives voiced similar arguments at the company's 2000 shareholder meeting. Shareholder Harrington Investments wanted to remove GM ingredients from the company's products. After vigorous debate, a majority of shareholders sided with company management. The shareholders rejected the proposed ban on GM ingredients.

People especially care about whether baby food is safe and pure. In 2000, Novartis A.G. announced that its prepared foods, including Gerber baby foods, would no longer contain GM ingredients. As it made that announcement, the agricultural division of the company still marketed GM seeds.

Pressure on companies continues. Activist groups such as Friends of the Earth, the Center for Food Safety, the Organic Consumers Association, Greenpeace, and the Pesticide Action Network urge consumers to write to companies. News stories raise consumer awareness too.

"I guarantee you, the food companies wish this issue would go away," food industry consultant Robert Golden told *The New York Times*.[9] If critics of genetically engineered foods have their way, the issue will not go away any time soon.

The Furor Abroad

In Montpelier, France, Greenpeace activists heaped tons of GM soy meal on top of an American flag. The activists were protesting American exports of GM food. They timed the protest to coincide with a biotechnology conference in the city.

In Genoa, Italy, four thousand protesters marched at the site of another biotechnology conference. Armed riot police were on hand to prevent violence.

During 1999, French farmers took their protests against GM food to McDonald's. They dumped heaps of manure and rotting produce in front of the restaurants.

Compared to the United States, some European countries are almost up in arms over genetically engineered food. Due to intense media coverage, many Europeans object when tests or research are carried out. They especially complain about GM crops developed by non-European companies. They fear that American businesses are profiting by foisting off unsafe products abroad.

As a result, European governments have been more reluctant than the United States to approve new GM foods. Some other countries have had similar responses, including Japan and Brazil.

Why should people view GM food so differently depending upon where they live? "Consumers in Europe think they're bearing all the risk with very little benefit," explains Ohio State University economist Ian Sheldon. "Most of the products out there at the moment are of benefit to farmers, notably in the U.S. European consumers feel they're taking risks in consuming these products and getting either no or very little benefit."[10]

People also view government differently. In the United States, people often disagree with regulatory agency actions. But disagreements are noted in publicly available files. And agencies usually make public the data on which they base their decisions. In other words, U.S. administrative agencies work mostly "in the open." In general, they have a strong record for regulating industry and watching out for health, safety, and environmental concerns. Thus, most citizens feel a certain level of trust. They believe the government is ultimately protecting them.

In contrast, most Europeans do not share that confidence. In general, says Sheldon, "Consumers in Europe do not believe what scientists and government tell them about food safety."[11]

Mad cow disease provides an example. Mad cow

disease is bovine spongiform encephalopathy. That nervous system disease affects cattle. In the late 1980s, people first worried whether livestock exposed to mad cow disease could transmit it to peo ple through the food chain. At first, European governments said not to worry.

Then, around 1996, the British government acknowledged there might be a link. Later data showed increases in Creutzfeldt-Jacob Disease (JCD). JCD is the equivalent of mad cow disease in humans. People felt shaken and dismayed. "For ten years we had been told this would not cause a problem for human beings," complained Sheila McKechnie of Britain's Consumer Association, "and then a [government] minister says, "Oh, dear, that wasn't true."[12]

Mad cow disease is an entirely separate issue from genetically engineered food. But many European consumers still feel wary about food safety. "I think that's generating part of the backlash against GMOs in the European Union," observes Sheldon. "They're uncertain about the risks. They don't want to take the risks. And they don't necessarily believe what scientists tell them."[13]

Thanks to the media, European consumers also know more about GM foods. In one poll, 90 percent of Europeans had heard or read about genetically engineered foods. One in three Americans knew nothing.[14]

Europeans' attitudes affect American business. Some companies have trouble finding foreign markets for surplus GM foods. That can mean less money flowing into the United States from abroad.

Do most people care about whether their food contains GM ingredients? Surveys show that Americans as a group feel less strongly about the issue than people in some other countries.

Other companies may sell only non-GM products in certain countries. Yet they can still find themselves in a bind.

Kellogg's, for example, stopped selling GM food in Europe. Meanwhile, its cereals sold in the United States could still contain GM ingredients. In December 2000, Greenpeace representatives visited company headquarters in Battle Creek, Michigan. One representative dressed up as FrankenTony—a mutant version of Kellogg's Tony the Tiger. Another dressed as Dr. Seuss's character, the Grinch. "Kellogg's is the grinch who stole breakfast!" the Grinch character said. "Americans should not have to worry about gene-contaminated corn when they buy Kellogg's cereal for their kids."[15]

Other countries get drawn into the fray. Thailand, for example, exports rice, shrimp, tapioca, coconut milk, and other foods. In 1999, the Thai government halted imports of GM seeds. European customers had said they did not want to buy genetically engineered foods. The Thai government wanted to make sure its farmers could sell their crops.

A different view does not mean that all European consumers are fearful. Nor does it mean that Americans are too trusting. Rather, different cultures affect whether people feel comfortable with possible new risks. Cultural factors affect how people view new technologies. And cultural factors definitely affect whether people are willing to pay for products of those new technologies.

Also, public opinion is not a matter of black and white. Even where cultural sentiments lean one way, people often have a range of opinions. Some Europeans do support GM food. Indeed, some European companies or their subsidiaries do business in food biotechnology. Some Americans are also wary of what government says about food safety. Like their European counterparts, these GM food critics do not want to trust someone else on issues of health and environmental safety.

7

An Ongoing Debate

They called themselves the Dusty Desperadoes. The police called them criminals. In July 2000, the group destroyed five acres of crops at a Monsanto test farm in Washington State. "Monsanto may have its capitalist spurs dug into our lives," read a message from the group, "but with machetes and scythes, we destroyed its attempt at corporate greenwashing by leveling five acres of field tests including some Roundup Ready canola."[1]

Vandalism is the willful destruction of property owned by someone else. Sometimes people commit vandalism for no obvious reason. Other times, frustrated groups do it to make a statement. In essence, vandals stop any debate and take matters into their own hands. Consider these examples:

Activists in Berkeley, California, called themselves Green Streets. The group attacked a GM corn test plot at the University of California at Berkeley. They ruined months of research.[2]

In Maine, another group hacked down over fifteen hundred GM trees at a Mead Corporation facility. "We will continue to stand up to corporate greed," declared a message from the vandals.[3]

In Hawaii, a group calling itself the Menehune struck. The name means "elves" or "little people" in the Hawaiian language. The group ruined a test plot of GM corn owned by Novartis. It also ruined test plots of papayas, pineapples, and other crops at the Kauai Agricultural Resource Center. The group's members wanted to keep genetically engineered food out of Hawaii. "You can feel the violence suffered by the 'Aina, the land, when you walk around here at night," said the group's message.[4]

On New Year's Eve 1999, a group calling itself the Earth Liberation Front (ELF) committed arson at Michigan State University. The fire destroyed offices of a university genetic engineering program. It caused $400,000 in damages.[5]

Other actions by the "elves" included destroying oat plants and gluing building locks at the University of Minnesota. The group committed arson at Boise Cascade offices in Oregon. It destroyed trees at a United States Forest Service research station in

Wisconsin. From 1997 through July 2000, the group claimed responsibility for causing over $31 million in damages.[6]

Vandalism, arson, and similar acts clearly violate the law. People committing the crimes want to stop GM food. Because the law allows it, the groups feel frustrated. They turn to illegal sabotage. The groups know that vandalism is a crime. They feel it is a lesser crime than their feared dangers of GM food. They claim that the feared risks somehow justify their crimes.

The groups also want media attention. That way they spread their message. They let others know that they think genetically engineered food is wrong.

But do two wrongs ever make a right? In 1999, police arrested England's Lord Peter Melchett and about thirty other people. Melchett was the executive director of Greenpeace in Great Britain. The group had destroyed GM corn in an English test field.

Walnut Tree Farm's owners had planted herbi-cide-tolerant corn for AgrEvo with the government's permission. But the vandals did not care about the government's permission. "These crops represent an unnecessary and unpredictable risk to the natural environment, which there is no justification for tak-ing," declared Melchett. "It's quite proper legally to remove that risk if it's the only course open."[7]

No one doubted that Melchett and the others committed the crime. Yet they were acquitted of criminal charges a year later. Trial testimony high-lighted the group's well-meaning intent. "I feel deeply I did the right thing," Melchett testified. "It was the only way to prevent the pollution of our environment by these dangerous organisms."[8]

Opponents of GM food liken attacks on GM food facilities to civil disobedience such as that used by Dr. Martin Luther King, Jr., and Mohandas K. Gandhi, who broke laws they believed to be immoral.

People who take "direct action" against genetic engineering stress that they do not use violence. But one day someone might get hurt. What if someone had been in one of the buildings the "elves" burned? Or suppose Walnut Tree Farm's owners and Melchett's group had come to blows?

Larger gatherings pose more risk. Angry protests by GM food foes, plus other groups, greeted the 1999 World Trade Organization meeting in Seattle. The crowd got so unruly that the city sent in riot police.

In any case, the law protects both people and their property. Vandals would certainly object if someone burned their office or ruined their gardens. People growing GM crops lawfully expect their property rights to be respected too.

Michael Fumento of the Hudson Institute says biovandalism shows "contempt for democracy."[9] The government that allows GM crops was elected by a majority of the voters. A minority of activists should not illegally overrule decisions by that government.

Vandalism causes political problems too. It aggravates tense trade relations where countries want to export GM crops. It can also alienate developing countries that want their people to grow GM crops.

They may resent "ecoterrorists" trying to deprive them of technology.

Ironically, vandalism can sometimes work against the things the vandals say they want. For example, critics often argue that not enough scientific testing has been done on genetically engineered foods. Then, saboteurs sometimes attack research in progress. In one incident, vandals attacked Scotland's only full-scale farm trial of GM canola.

"Even environmental groups agree that widespread testing has to be carried out on GM technology if we are to progress further," announced Scottish Parliament representative Nora Radcliffe. "This unnecessary action by individuals with an extremist agenda serves no purpose whatsoever."[10]

Vandalism also cuts off discussion. Vandals say they are protecting the environment. But farmers like Walnut Tree Farm's William Brigham feel that using less herbicide helps the environment.[11] When groups resort to vandalism, neither side wants to listen to the other.

Lawlessness also undermines groups' credibility with the public. "If you go too far," warned GM critic Jeremy Rifkin, "nobody pays attention."[12]

Arrogant Attitudes

Companies have sometimes fanned the fires in the GM food debate. At first Monsanto proceeded slowly. During the 1980s, it planned to reach out to government regulators, farmers, and other groups. It wanted their support for genetically engineered food.

Then in the 1990s, the company switched policy. It wanted products approved and gotten to market quickly. Instead of a soft, slow approach, it was full steam ahead. When critics voiced concerns, the company was more likely to dismiss them than to address them.

"We've learned that there is often a very fine line between scientific confidence on the one hand and corporate arrogance on the other," admitted Robert Shapiro.[13] Shapiro was chairman of Monsanto Company before the company's merger with Pharmacia Corporation.

Before the merger, Shapiro spoke to the Greenpeace Business Conference in London. "We've tended to see it as our task to convince people that this is a good, useful technology; to convince people, in short, that we are right and that by extension people who have different points of view are wrong—or at best misguided." Shapiro urged people to view genetic engineering as a tool. "Like most tools, like most scientific knowledge, biotechnology in itself is neither good nor bad," Shapiro stressed. "It can be used well, or it can be used badly. Like any important new tool, it creates new choices for society."[14]

The comments sounded conciliatory. But were they too little, too late? "For the price of what it would have cost to market a new breakfast cereal, the biotech industry probably could have saved itself a lot of the struggle that it is going through today," Gene Grabowski told *The New York Times*. Grabowski represented the Grocery Manufacturers of America.[15]

Yet the GM food debate is more than a public relations problem. Other groups echo comments that genetic engineering is a tool that should be examined on a case-by-case basis. The Union of Concerned Scientists, for example, says it prefers to look at each case's risks and benefits.[16]

In practice, the group's statements suggest that they believe GM foods' benefits would rarely, if ever, outweigh the risks. Even many field trials do not necessarily show that a crop is environmentally safe. The group feels that environmental risks are global—not local.

Greenpeace also has said it does not oppose genetic engineering per se. It accepts various medical uses of the technology. It may also accept limited uses in greenhouses.

But Greenpeace seems to draw the line at open field testing and planting. That amounts to an "environmental release" of GM organisms.[17] Friends of the Earth has voiced similar views.

Of course, most food grows outdoors. Thus, these critics oppose almost all uses of genetic engineering for food.

In short, both sides' rhetoric sounds similar. Their statements sound similar. Many of their terms even have similar meaning. But their bottom-line positions differ tremendously.

Still, the important step is starting a dialogue. Ideally, that dialogue will involve many groups: activist organizations, companies that develop foods, universities and researchers, government regulators, farmers, food marketers, and consumers. Probably no one will be happy with every decision. But dialogue can help all groups explore potential benefits and pitfalls of genetically engineered food. With luck, people can minimize risks and maximize potential benefits.

Acting on Incomplete Information

Is GM food safe? Incomplete information makes it hard to give an absolute answer.

Scientists have already done many studies on genetically engineered foods. Studies can give a lot of comfort. Yet studies take place under carefully controlled conditions. The real world is not easily controlled.

These USDA scientists are growing genetically engineered potato plants. "Ecoterrorists" have sometimes destroyed plants used for research on the safety of GM food.

By design, scientific studies answer only specific questions. Does a certain GM crop require more or less pesticide than a comparable non-GM crop? How does a certain GM food differ chemically from a comparable non-GM food when exposed to stomach acid? Do fields planted with a certain GM crop have more or less of certain insects than comparable non-GM crop fields? And so on.

No single study tells whether GM foods are safe. More generally, science cannot "prove a negative." Studies can say whether data support a specific hypothesis. But not proving a specific risk is different from saying that there is no risk at all.

Many scientists are also cautious by nature. They feel comfortable reporting on what specific studies show. In contrast, they feel uncomfortable making generalizations that cannot be proved by specific data. Some scientists may feel that certain risks are minimal. Few are ready to give guarantees that nothing will ever go wrong.

People can also question studies' validity for a number of reasons. If a company or an activist group pays for a study, the other side may claim bias. Lack of peer review may also cause criticism. (In peer review, other scientific professionals critique a paper before it gets published.) In order to protect business interests, many studies submitted for government review are not published. Thus, they may lack formal peer review.

"We're a ways away from really having answers," announced ecologist LaReesa Wolfenbarger.[18] In an article published in the journal *Science*, she and biologist Paul Phifer concluded that existing studies could not answer whether GM crops are safe for the environment. More studies should be done, they said.[19]

Of course, studies cost money. The total bill to study Bt crops' possible effects on butterflies could range between $2 million and $3 million. That exceeds USDA's average annual grant awards for studying environmental risk.[20] Plus, the butterfly issue is just one question. Dozens of other issues remain.

"We've got only so much time and energy and resources to devote to risk assessment and risk management," notes Adrianne Massey in North Carolina.[21] GM food supporters say they are perfectly willing to study reasonable risks. But at some point they question whether critics' worries become unreasonable. Plus, genetically engineered food is not the only subject that raises questions about potential risk.

Critics, on the other hand, do not accept those explanations. Critics worry whether GM food will harm the earth's environment forever. They worry about possible health effects too. For them, a "wait and see" approach is not acceptable. Plus, critics of GM food do not trust companies to do the right thing.

What Are the Alternatives?

People who oppose genetically engineered food can try to avoid it, but they pay a price. First, those consumers must spend more time reading labels. Some companies might say whether their foods have GM ingredients. Alternatively, consumers wary about GM foods could choose certified organic foods. Is organic food better?

Greenpeace and other groups say organic farming helps the environment. They also feel that organic foods avoid any potential questions about safety of GM foods or foods grown with man-made chemicals or fertilizers.

Other people say organic food is no healthier than regular food or genetically engineered food. David Lineback of the University of Maryland's Joint Institute for Food Safety and Applied Nutrition maintains that organic foods provide no special health or safety benefits. Plus, he argues, some "natural" pesticides used by organic farmers pose potential health and environmental problems too.[22]

Where Do You Stand?

"Before accepting or condemning a new technology, consider both the pros and the cons," advises Alan McHughen at the University of Saskatchewan. "Obtain factual information and debate both sides of the argument."[23]

People base their beliefs about GM food on many factors. Some rely on their understanding of science. Others focus more broadly on social issues. Some people are naturally cautious and hesitant about new technology. Others are more willing to experiment until facts prove there is a problem. Many people also rely on an instinctive feeling about what seems right or wrong.

Gender may also play a role in people's feelings. In December 2000, *USA Today* reported that women were generally more skeptical about GM food. While 71 percent of men surveyed said they would eat genetically engineered food, only 50 percent of women would. Thirty-five percent of men surveyed said they would pay more for non-GM food. For women the figure was 47 percent—nearly half.[24] Of course, most people surveyed probably were already eating GM food. Remember that GM ingredients are in roughly two thirds of supermarket foods already.

Survey results also differ based on how questions are asked. In 2001, the International Food Information Council Federation (IFIC) released its own survey figures. It showed that only 2 percent of American consumers worried about whether genetically engineered food was safe.[25] Obviously, the surveys had dramatically different results.

Levels of consumer acceptance will ultimately affect the food industry's use of GM ingredients. Increased government regulation, foreign trade relations, and other issues may factor in too.

Meanwhile, each person faces personal decisions. How do you feel about GM food? What, if any, actions are you willing to take in response?

The first step is evaluating all available evidence. "Consider not only the consequences of adopting the new technology," says McHughen. "Consider the consequences of NOT adopting the technology. After all, the current practice, the status quo, is what got us to where we are."[26]

Try to avoid prejudices when forming an opinion. As Joe Schwarcz of McGill University's chemistry department points out, just because something is good for big corporations does not mean that it is automatically bad for everyone else.[27] Likewise, do not assume that one side is scientific and the other side is not. Supporters and critics of genetically engineered food both cite scientific data for their positions. And both sides raise some valid points.

Also realize that almost nothing in life is risk free. "Never put off doing something useful for fear of evil that may never arrive," said James Watson, who discovered DNA's structure with Francis Crick.[28] But knowing about risks is important. Knowledge can let people take reasonable steps to avoid serious harm.

When you decide how you feel about genetically engineered food, make your views known. Federal agencies invite members of the public to comment on proposed rules. Notice of these opportunities appears in the *Federal Register*. News articles or agency Web sites may also publicize proposed agency actions. Members of Congress welcome letters from constituents.

Letters to the newspaper provide another way to voice opinions. Letters will more likely get printed if they are short and to the point. A good letter to the editor also notes facts that support its position.

People can get involved with groups that share their views. Many organizations welcome volunteers. Most gladly accept financial contributions too.

Young people on both sides of the debate can also put their talents to work. Study biology, chemistry, genetics, mathematics, and related subjects to build a good foundation in science. Students who believe that GM food offers huge promise for feeding the world's people can explore careers in biotechnology. Students who worry about GM food can explore careers that will make other alternatives more attractive.

In the fairy tale "Snow White," the wicked queen tempted Snow White with a juicy red apple. The fruit looked delicious and healthful. In fact, it turned out to be poisonous. Genetically engineered food looks as if it offers many promises. Yet critics worry that it may be even more dangerous than the fairy tale apple. Critics fear that GM food could hurt not only the people who eat it, but also the ecological balance of the entire world. Critics worry not only about our food today, but also about the future of the world's food supply for generations to come.

Are genetically engineered foods good for the world's people? Or should people be wary of them? Experts on both sides will debate the pros and cons of GM food for years to come.

An old saying holds, "You are what you eat." Think carefully about the food in your diet. Think too about how the world will feed all its people. Whether GM food helps or hurts humanity depends on what we can learn about it and the actions we take.

Chapter Notes

Chapter 1. Food Fights

1. Jeffrey Kluger, "Watchdogs Who Bite," *Time*, February 7, 2000, p. 67; Sarah Ramose, "Protests Greet Biodiversity Summit," *The Lancet*, January 29, 2000, p. 386.

2. Brian O'Reilly, "Reaping a Biotech Blunder," *Fortune*, February 19, 2001, p. 156; Marc Kaufman, "2nd Study Links Gene-Altered Corn, Butterfly Deaths," *Washington Post*, August 22, 2000, p. A2.

3. John E. Losey, Linda S. Rayor, and Maureen E. Carter, "Transgenic Pollen Harms Monarch Larvae," *Nature*, May 20, 1999, p. 214.

4. Scott Kilman, "U.S. Farmers Cutting Back on Crops That Have Been Genetically Modified," *Wall Street Journal*, April 3, 2000, p. A4; "Whither GM Corn?" *Environment*, December 1999, p. 9.

5. John E. Beringer, "Cautionary Tale on Safety of GM Crops," *Nature*, June 3, 1999, p. 405; "Monarch Butterflies and Bt Corn," 1999–2000, <http://www.bio.org/food&ag/butterfly.htm> (January 7, 2002).

6. Stephen J. Milloy, "Study Eases Gene-Altered Corn Fears," *Chicago Sun-Times*, November 4, 1999, p. 57.

7. "Absence of Toxicity of Bacillus Thuringiensis Pollen to Black Swallowtails Under Field Conditions," *Proceedings of National Academy of Sciences*, vol. 97, no. 14, 7700-03 (July 5, 2000); Carol Kaesuk Yoon, "Type of Biotech Corn Found to Be Safe to a Butterfly Species," *The New York Times*, June 6, 2000, p. D2 (N), F2(L).

8. Kaufman.

9. Biotechnology Industry Organization, "BIO Statement Regarding Purported New Findings on BT Corn and Monarch Butterflies," press release, August 21, 2000, <http://www.bio.org/news/article.html> (August 23, 2000); Biotechnology Industry Organization, "EPA Report

Finds Biotech Crops Have Little Impact on Monarch Butterflies," press release, October 19, 2000.

10. U.S. EPA, "Bt Plant-Pesticides Biopesticides Registration Action Document," October 2000, p. 12, <http://www.epa.gov/scipoly/sap> (February 15, 2001).

11. FIFRA Scientific Advisory Panel, "Sets of Scientific Issues Being Considered by the Environmental Protection Agency Regarding: Bt Plant-Pesticides Risk and Benefit Assessments," *SAP Report* No. 2000-07, March 12, 2001, <http://www.epa.gov/scipoly/sap/2000/october/octoberfinal.pdf> (March 18, 2001).

12. Michelle Healy, "Biotech Corn Doesn't Hurt Butterflies," *USA Today*, September 11, 2001, p. 7D.

13. Donald G. McNeil, "Redesigning Nature: A Reign of Fear," *The New York Times*, March 14, 2000, p. A1; David Barboza, "Modified Foods Put Companies in a Quandary," *The New York Times*, June 4, 2000, p 1.

14. Lucette Lagnado, "Group Sows Seeds of Revolt Against Genetically Altered Foods in U.S.," *Wall Street Journal*, October 12, 1999, p. B2; Biotechnology Industry Organization, "BIO Statement Regarding Purported New Findings on BT Corn and Monarch Butterflies."

15. Lagnado.

16. "Acres of the World's Farmland Sown with Genetically Modified Food," *USA Today*, February 11, 2000, p. 1A.

17. David Barboza, "Farmers Favor Genetically Altered Crops, Producers Say," *The New York Times*, February 13, 2001, p. C2; Jeff Wheelwright, "Don't Eat Again Until You Read This," *Discover*, March 2001, p. 36.

Chapter 2. How Genetic Engineering Works

1. Personal interview with David Francis, Ph.D., Ohio State University, September 28, 2000.

2. Personal interview with John Finer, Ph.D., Ohio State University, September 28, 2000.

3. Telephone interview with Adrianne Massey, Ph.D., December 5, 2000.

4. Ibid.

Chapter 3. Why GM Food?

1. "High-Protein Corn Developed in Mexico," *USA Today*, September 12, 2000, p. 6D.

2. Biotechnology Industry Organization, *Editors' & Reporters' Guide to Biotechnology*, 5th ed., June 2001, <http://www.bio.org/aboutbio/guide2001/letter.pdf> (September 6, 2001); Norman Borlaug, "We Need Biotech to Feed the World," *Wall Street Journal*, December 6, 2000, p. A22.

3. E-mail communication with Alan McHughen, Ph.D., senior research scientist, University of Saskatchewan, Dec. 12, 2000.

4. Biotechnology Industry Organization.

5. Ibid.

6. Borlaug.

7. Jane Rissler and Margaret Mellon, *The Ecological Risks of Engineered Crops* (Cambridge, Mass.: MIT Press, 1996), pp. 19–20.

8. Anuradha Mittal and Peter Rosset, "There Is Food for All: Access Is the Problem," *Wall Street Journal*, December 21, 2000, p. A19; Michel Bessieres, "GMOs: The Wrong Answer to the Wrong Problem," *UNESCO Courier*, January 2001, p. 30.

9. C.S. Prakash, "We Can Win the War Against Hunger," *Wall Street Journal*, January 2, 2001, p. A23.

10. McHughen.

11. Hassan Adamu, "We'll Feed Our People As We See Fit," *Washington Post*, September 11, 2000, p. A23. See also Andrew Pollack, "A Food Fight for High Stakes," *The New York Times*, Feb. 4, 2001, p. WK6.

12. Craig S. Smith, "China Rushes to Adopt Genetically Modified Crops," *The New York Times*,

October 7, 2000, p. A3; "The Voice of Reason in the Global Food Fight," *Fortune*, February 21, 2000, p. 164.

13. Jon Christensen, "Golden Rice in a Grenade-Proof Greenhouse," *The New York Times*, Nov. 21, 2000, p. F1.

14. Quirin Schlermeier, "Designer Rice To Combat Diet Deficiencies Makes Its Debut," *Nature*, February 1, 2001, p. 551; Monsanto Company, press release, August 4, 2000, <http://www.monsanto.com/monsanto/mediacenter/2000/00aug4_goldenrice.html> (September 12, 2001).

15. Christensen; Ganapati Mudur, "India's Plans To Grow GM Crops Draw Flak," *British Medical Journal*, January 20, 2001, p. 126.

16. Greenpeace, "GE Rice Is Fool's Gold," press release, February 9, 2001, <http://www.greenpeace.org/~geneng1/highlights/food/goldenrice.htm> (February 26, 2001); Michael Pollan, "The Great Yellow Hype," *The New York Times*, March 4, 2001, sec. 6, p. 15.

17. Gordon Conway, "Grain of Hope," *The Guardian*, March 21, 2001, p. 19.

18. "High-Protein Corn Developed in Mexico."

19. Rick Weiss, "Biotech Research Branches Out," *Washington Post*, August 3, 2000, p. A1.

20. E-mail communication with Neal Carter, Okanagan Biotechnology, Inc., September 9, 2001.

21. National Institute of Allergy and Infectious Diseases, "First Human Trial Shows that an Edible Vaccine is Feasible," press release, April 27, 1998, <http://www.niaid.nih.gov/newsroom/releases/ediblevacc.htm> (January 7, 2002).

22. Bill Sloat, "Biting a Banana May Replace Shot; Potato Tests Show Concept Works," *Cleveland Plain Dealer*, May 8, 2000, p. 1F.

23. Robert Paarlberg, "The Global Food Fight," *Foreign Affairs*, May–June 2000, p. 24.

24. Ibid.; Brian O'Reilly, "Reaping a Biotech Blunder," *Fortune*, February 19, 2001, p. 156.

25. Personal interview with Joseph Kovach, Ph.D., Ohio State University, September 28, 2000.

26. Ibid.

27. Ibid.

28. Telephone interview with Adrianne Massey, Ph.D., December 5, 2000; Monsanto, "Glyphosate Health and Safety," March 22, 2000, <http://www.monsanto. com/monsanto/media/backgrounders/00mar22_ glyhealth.html> (January 7, 2002).

29. Massey.

30. LaReesa Wolfenbarger and Paul Phifer, "The Ecological Risks and Benefits of Genetically Engineered Plants," *Science*, December 15, 2000, p. 2088; Carol Kaesuk Yoon, "Gene-Altered Crop Studies Are Called Inconclusive," *The New York Times*, December 14, 2000, p. A22(E).

31. McHughen.

32. Ibid.

Chapter 4. A Frightening Harvest?

1. Prince Charles, "Seeds of Disaster," *The Daily Telegraph*, June 8, 1998, <http://193.36.68.132/ speeches/agriculture_08061998.html> (February 15, 2001); Warren Hoge, "Britain's Green Prince and His Family Differ on Altered Crops," *The New York Times*, June 7, 2000, p. A19; Nigel Williams, "Agricultural Biotech Faces Backlash in Europe," *Science*, August 7, 1998, p. 768.

2. "Quotable Quotes from Scientists and Other Folks on the Dangers of Gentically Engineered Food and Crops," *Organic Consumers Association Page*, n.d., <http://www. purefood.org/ge/sciquotes.htm> (December 28, 2000).

3. Ibid.

4. Ibid.

5. Luke Anderson, *Genetic Engineering, Food, and Our Environment* (White River Junction, Vt.: Chelsea Green Publishing Co., 2000), pp. 13–14; Eric S. Grace,

Biotechnology Unzipped: Promises & Realities (Washington, D.C.: Joseph Henry Press), pp. 88–90.

6. Alan McHughen, *Pandora's Picnic Basket: The Potential and Hazards of Genetically Modified Foods* (New York: Oxford University Press, 2000), pp. 114–117; Grace, pp. 88–90.

7. Stanley Ewen and Arpad Pusztai, "Effect of Diets Containing Genetically Modified Potatoes Expressing Galanthus Nivalis Lectin on Rat Small Intestine," *The Lancet*, October 16, 1999, p. 1353; Allan Mowat, et al., "GM Food Debate," *The Lancet*, November 13, 1999, p. 1725; Richard Horton, "Genetically Modified Foods: 'Absurd' Concern or Welcome Dialogue?" *The Lancet*, October 16, 1999, p. 1314; McHughen, *Pandora's Picnic Basket*, pp. 117–118, 141–143.

8. Letter from Helen B. Palmer to FDA Commissioner Jane Henney, FDA Docket 99N-4282, November 17, 1999, <http://www.fda.gov/ohrms/dockets/dockets/99n4282/c000081.pdf> (January 7, 2002).

9. "Frankenfoods Are Good for You," *Wall Street Journal*, October 20, 1999, p. A27.

10. Ibid.

11. Marc Kaufman, "Biotech Crops Appear Safe, Panel Says," *Washington Post*, April 6, 2000, p. A10; Laura Tangley, "Of Genes, Grain, and Grocers," *U.S. News & World Report*, April 10, 2000, p. 49.

12. Robyn Suriano, "Genetic Engineering: AMA Panel says Biotech Food Safe," *Knight-Ridder/Tribune News Service*, December 5, 2000.

13. Tom Spears, "'Superweeds' Invade Farm Fields," *Ottawa Citizen*, February 6, 2001, p. A6.

14. M.J. Crawley, et al., "Transgenic Crops in Natural Habitats," *Nature*, February 8, 2001, p. 682.

15. Paul Sletten, letter to USDA, Docket #FGIS-2000-001A, November 30, 2000.

16. Jeremy Rifkin, *The Biotech Century: Harnessing the Gene and Remaking the World* (New York: Jeremy P. Tarcher/Putnam, 1998), pp. 98–99; Robin Mather, *A*

Garden of Unearthly Delights: Bioengineering and the Future of Food (New York: Dutton, 1995), pp. 14–15.

17. Michael W. Fox, *Beyond Evolution: The Genetically Altered Future of Plants, Animals, the Earth . . . and Humans* (New York: Lyons Press, 1999), pp. 103–105.

18. Times Wire Services, "Monsanto Says 2001 Profits Are Due To Rise," *Los Angeles Times*, February 13, 2001, p. C7.

19. Stephen Nottingham, *Eat Your Genes: How Genetically Modified Food Is Entering Our Diet* (London & New York: Zed Books, Ltd., 1998), pp. 108–110; Daniel Callahan, "Food for Thought," *Commonweal*, April 7, 2000, p. 7.

20. "Quotable Quotes from Scientists and Other Folks on the Dangers of Genetically Engineered Food and Crops."

21. Elizabeth M. Whelan, *Toxic Terror* (Buffalo, N.Y.: Prometheus Books, 1993), pp. 100–105.

Chapter 5. Government's Role

1. Dan Glickman, "How Will Scientists, Farmers, and Consumers Learn to Love Biotechnology and What Happens If They Don't?" remarks to National Press Club, July 13, 1999, <http://www.usda.gov/news/releases/1999/07/0285> (December 17, 2000).

2. Ann M. Veneman, statement at UN Food and Agriculture Organization 31st Conference, Plenary Session: State of Food and Agriculture, Rome, Italy, November 5, 2001, <http://www.usda.gov/agencies/biotech/role.html> (March 27, 2002).

3. U.S. Department of Agriculture.

4. Joseph A. Levitt, Statement Before the Health, Education, Labor, and Pensions Committee of the United States Senate, September 26, 2000, <http://www.cfsan.fda.gov/~lrd/stbioeng.html> (January 7, 2002); Larry Thompson, "Are Bioengineered Foods Safe?" *FDA Consumer*, January–February 2000, p. 18.

5. FDA, "FDA Announces Proposal and Draft Guidance for Food Developed Through Biotechnology,"

press release, January 17, 2001, <http://www.fda.gov/bbs/topics/NEWS/2001/NEW000747.html> (January 17, 2001).

6. Grocery Manufacturers of America, "FDA Proposal for Biotech Labeling and Product Approval 'A Victory for Consumers,'" press release, January 17, 2001; Andrew Pollack, "F.D.A. Plans New Scrutiny in Areas of Biotechnology," *The New York Times*, January 18, 2001, p. A12(E).

7. Biotechnology Industry Organization, "BIO Supportive of FDA Announcement on Biotech Foods," press release, January 17, 2001.

8. Telephone interview with Charles Margulis, Greenpeace USA, January 23, 2001.

9. Marc Kaufman, "FDA Issues Biotech Food Rules," *Washington Post*, January 18, 2001, p. E3.

10. Public Interest Research Group, "New FDA Policy Fails to Require Testing or Labeling of Genetically Engineered Food," press release, January 17, 2001, <http://www.pirg.org/ge/press/newfdapolicy.html> (January 20, 2001).

11. Letter from Beverly Stewart to U.S. Department of Agriculture, FGIS-2000-001a, December 13, 2000.

12. Letter from Patrick Moore to FDA Commissioner Jane Henney, Docket 99N-4282, December 23, 1999, <http://www.fda.gov/ohrms/dockets/dockets/99/n/4282/c000511.pdf> (January 11, 2001).

13. E-mail from Tanya M. Russ to U.S. Department of Agriculture, FGIS-2000-001a, December 9, 2000.

14. Sarah Lueck and Scott Kilman, "Gene-Altered Food Needs Labels, Safety Reviews, Committee Says," *Wall Street Journal*, December 19, 2000, p. B6; Marian Burros, "Labeling Foods With Designer Genes," *The New York Times*, January 3, 2001, p. F2(E).

15. Andrew Bard Schmookler, "Label Modified Food? Of Course," *Christian Science Monitor*, April 18, 2000, p. 9.

16. Kurt Eichenwald, Gina Kolata, and Melody Petersen, "Biotechnology Food: From the Lab to a Debacle," *The New York Times*, January 25, 2001, p. A1.

17. Telephone interview with Adrianne Massey, Ph.D., December 5, 2000.

18. Ibid.

19. Telephone interview with Ian Sheldon, Ph.D., Ohio State University, September 27, 2000.

20. Ibid.

21. U.S. Department of Agriculture, "Glickman Announces National Standards for Organic Food," press release, December 20, 2000, <http://www.usda.gov/news/releases/2000/12/0425.htm> (January 3, 2001); Marc Kaufman, "U.S. Sets 'Organic' Standard," *Washington Post*, December 21, 2000, p. A1.

22. Personal interview with David Francis, Ph.D., Ohio State University, September 28, 2000.

23. Eli Kintisch, "Sticker Shock: Why Label Food?" *The New Republic*, January 22, 2001, p. 12.

24. FDA, "Guidance for Industry: Voluntary Labeling Indicating Whether Foods Have or Have Not Been Developed Using Bioengineering," draft, January 2001, <http://www.fda.gov/OHRMS/DOCKETS/98fr/001598gd.pdf> (January 17, 2001); FDA, Notice of Availability, 66 *Federal Register* 4839 (January 18, 2001).

25. Grocery Manufacturers of America.

26. Margulis.

27. Anita Manning, "Taco Bell Asked to Hold the Chalupas," *USA Today*, September 19, 2000, p. 1D.

28. Andrew Pollack, "Plan for Use of Bioengineered Corn in Food Is Disputed," *The New York Times*, November 29, 2000, p. C4(E).

29. Ibid.

30. Andrew Pollack, "Case Illustrates Risks of Altered Food," *The New York Times*, October 14, 2000, p. A13(E).

31. Ibid.

32. U.S. Environmental Protection Agency, "Statement by Stephen Johnson EPA Deputy Assistant Administrator for Pesticides Regarding StarLink Corn," press release, October 19, 2000.

33. Pollack, "Case Illustrates Risks of Altered Food."

34. Centers for Disease Control and Prevention, "Investigation of Human Health Effects Associated with Potential Exposure to Genetically Modified Corn," 2001, <http://www.cdc.gov/nceh/ehhe/Cry9cReport/default.htm> (September 7, 2001); Jeff Wheelwright, "Don't Eat Again Until You Read This," *Discover*, March 2001, p. 36.

35. U.S. Environmental Protection Agency; Brian O'Reilly, "Reaping a Biotech Blunder," *Fortune*, February 19, 2001, p. 156.

36. David Barboza, "Negligence Suit Is Filed Over Altered Corn," *The New York Times*, December 4, 2000, p. C2(E).

37. Justin Gillis and Greg Schneider, "Firm Will Pay Corn Farmers," *Washington Post*, January 24, 2001, p. E1; Associated Press, "Reimbursement for Altered Corn," *The New York Times*, January 24, 2001, p. C16(E).

38. Burros.

39. Consumer Federation of America, "Report Says U.S. Regulation of Genetically Modified Foods Includes Huge Loopholes that Permit Marketing with Little Government Oversight," press release, January 11, 2001.

40. Anthony Shadid, "The Seeds of Science: EPA To Finish Review of Major Genetically Engineered Crops, Decide Their Future," *Boston Globe*, March 7, 2001, p. D4.

Chapter 6. To Market, to Market

1. Union of Concerned Scientists, "Post-Approval Blues: FlavrSavr Tomato—Squashed," *The Gene Exchange*, Fall 1997, <http://www.ucsusa.org/Gene/F97/agribusiness.html> (December 12, 2000); Luke Anderson, *Genetic Engineering, Food, and Our Environment* (White River Junction, Vt.: Chelsea Green Publishing Co., 2000), pp. 44–45.

2. Tony Spleen, "Altered Stakes: FDA Has Approved Calgene's Genetically Engineered Tomato, But Will Consumers Approve?" *Supermarket News*, August 22, 1994, p. 19.

3. Alan McHughen, *Pandora's Picnic Basket: The Potential and Hazards of Genetically Modified Foods* (New York: Oxford University Press, 2000), pp. 157–158; Spleen.

4. Elizabeth M. Whelan, "Scientists Embrace Food Biotechnology, But Some Food Companies Run for Cover," American Council on Science and Health Editorial, March 1, 2000, <http://www.acsh.org/press/editorials/biotechnology030200> (July 10, 2000).

5. Andrew Pollack, "Novartis Ended Use of Gene-Altered Foods," *The New York Times*, August 4, 2000, p. C4(E).

6. Laura Tangley, "Of Genes, Grain, and Grocers," *U.S. News & World Report*, April 10, 2000, p. 49.

7. Whelan.

8. Andrew Pollack, "Food Companies Urged to End Use of Biotechnology Products," *The New York Times*, July 20, 2000, p. C6(E).

9. David Barboza, "Modified Foods Put Companies in a Quandary," *The New York Times*, June 4, 2000, p. 1.1(E).

10. Telephone interview with Ian Sheldon, Ph.D., September 27, 2000.

11. Ibid.

12. Marc Champion, "Britons View Science Skeptically As Mad-Cow Report Is Released," *Wall Street Journal*, October 26, 2000, p. A23.

13. Sheldon; Emma Plugge, "The Paradoxes of Genetically Modified Foods," *British Medical Journal*, June 19, 1999, p. 1,694.

14. "Blech," *Economist*, January 15, 2000, p. 69.

15. Greenpeace, "The Grinch and Frankentony Return Gene-Altered Starlink Corn to Kellogg's," press release, December 20, 2000, <http://www.greenpeace.org/

~geneng/highlights/food/00_12_21.htm> (January 16, 2001).

Chapter 7. An Ongoing Debate

1. Genetix Alert, "Dusty Desperadoes Raid Monsanto," news release, August 1, 2000, <http://tao. ca/~ban/800ARdusty.htm> (March 1, 2001).

2. Genetix, "Green Streets Destroy Genetically Engineered Corn at UC Berkeley," press release, October 11, 2000, <http://tao.ca/~ban/1000ARgreenstreets.htm> (March 1, 2001).

3. Genetix, "Activists Destroy 1500-2000 GE Trees at MEAD Corporation Facilities," press release, July 25, 2000, <http://tao.ca/~ban/700ARmilo.htm> (March 1, 2001).

4. Genetix, "Hawaiian Elves Destroy GE Crops and Research on Island of Kauai," press release, May 2000, <http://tao.ca/~ban/500ARhawaii.htm> (March 1, 2001).

5. Francis X. Donnelly, "Genetically Altered Food: Safe or Threat? Worldwide War Hits Home as Research at MSU Spurs Vandalism," *Detroit News*, February 6, 2000, p. A1; Brad Knickerbocker, "Concerns Rise as Ecoterrorists Expand Aim," *Christian Science Monitor*, April 3, 2000, p. 3.

6. North American Earth Liberation Front, "Earth Liberation Front (ELF) Claims Responsibility for Sabotage at U.S. Forest Service's North Central Research Station Forest Biotechnology Laboratory," press release, July 20, 2000, <http://tao.ca/~ban/700ARforestlab.htm> (March 1, 2001).

7. James Cox, "Farm Owners Passionately Defend Crops," *USA Today*, January 31, 2000, p. 2B; Greenpeace, "Greenpeace Decontaminates GM Field— Lord Melchett Arrested," press release, July 26, 1999, <http://www.greenpeace.org/pressreleases/geneng/1999jul26.html> (March 1, 2001).

8. T.R. Reid, "Altered Crops on Trial in Britain," *Washington Post*, April 16, 2000, p. A31; Paul Kelso,

"Greenpeace Wins Key Case," *The Guardian*, September 21, 2000, p. 1; Greenpeace, "Greenpeace Volunteers Acquitted at GE Trial," press release, September 20, 2000, <http://www.greenpeace.org/~geneng/highlights/gmo/00_09_20.htm> (September 29, 2000).

9. Michael Fumento, "Crop Busters," *Reason*, January 2000, p. 44; Cox, p. 1B.

10. Frank Urquhart, "Protesters Hit GM Crop a Second Time," *The Scotsman*, July 11, 2000, p. 9.

11. Cox; Fumento, p. 44.

12. Jeffrey Kluger, "Watchdogs Who Bite," *Time*, February 7, 2000, p. 67.

13. Kurt Eichenwald, Gina Kolata, and Melody Petersen, "Biotechnology Food: From the Lab to a Debacle," *The New York Times*, January 25, 2001, p. A1.

14. Robert B. Shapiro, Monsanto chairman, address to Greenpeace Business Conference, October 6, 1999, <http://www.monsanto.com/monsanto/mediacenter/speeches/99oct6_Shapiroscript.html> (September 12, 2000).

15. Eichenwald, Kolata, and Petersen.

16. Jane Rissler and Margaret Mellon, *The Ecological Risks of Engineered Crops* (Cambridge, Mass.: MIT Press, 1996), p. 20.

17. Telephone interview with Charles Margulis, Greenpeace USA, January 23, 2001.

18. Carol Kaesuk Yoon, "Gene-Altered Crop Studies Are Called Inconclusive," *The New York Times*, December 14, 2000, p. A22(E).

19. LaRessa Wolfenbarger and Paul Phifer, "The Ecological Risks and Benefits of Genetically Engineered Plants," *Science*, December 15, 2000, p. 2088.

20. Carol Kaesuk Yoon, "What's Next for Biotech Crops?" *The New York Times*, December 19, 2000, p. F1(E).

21. Telephone interview with Adrianne Massey, Ph.D., December 5, 2000.

22. David Longtin and David Lineback, "Keep Eyes Open If You Go Organic," *USA Today*, January 24, 2001, p. 11A.

23. E-mail communication with Alan McHughen, Ph.D., senior research scientist, University of Saskatchewan, December 12, 2000.

24. "Genetically Altered Food: Women More Skeptical," *USA Today*, December 20, 2000, p. 1A.

25. Bill Hord, "Biotech Isn't Dead, Grain Handlers Told," *Omaha World-Herald*, February 16, 2001, p. 20.

26. McHughen.

27. Joe Schwarcz, "The Frankenfuror: Genetically Altered Crops Are the Biggest Hot Potato Since Pasteurization," *The* (Montreal) *Gazette*, November 12, 2000, p. C4.

28. Michael Jacobean, "Consumer Groups Shouldn't Reject Biotech," *Wall Street Journal*, January 25, 2001, p. A20.

Glossary

biotechnology—Manipulation of living organisms for human purposes. Development of GM foods is part of biotechnology.

chromosome—Molecule of DNA within a cell's nucleus that contains genes.

crossbreeding—Developing new varieties of food by selectively mating parents with particular traits.

DNA (deoxyribonucleic acid)—Chemical whose special arrangement of atom groups spells out the genetic code for an organism.

expressed—In genetics, a condition where a genetic trait is activated, or "turned on."

genetic engineering—Manipulating an organism's DNA, often to produce a GM organism.

genetically modified (GM)—Descriptive term for organisms whose DNA has been changed through transfer of one or more genes obtained from another species. Synonyms include "genetically engineered," "transgenic," and "genetically altered."

herbicide—Weed killer.

hybrid—Variety of plant developed through crossbreeding.

integrated pest management—Use of a variety of techniques to manage pests that aims to minimize harm to health and the environment. Techniques include rotating crops, intercropping, encouraging beneficial insects, and ensuring that any chemicals used have fewer health and environmental problems than alternatives.

marker gene—Gene included in a DNA package so scientists can determine which cells have incorporated the DNA package after a transfer.

monoculture—Practice of planting primarily one variety of a crop over a large area.

mutation—Change in an organism's DNA. Mutations can occur spontaneously, or scientists can induce mutations in the laboratory.

organic farming—Agriculture that avoids use of manmade fertilizers, herbicides, and pesticides. Most organic farmers do not grow GM foods.

patent—Limited monopoly to use, produce, and license a technology, which has been granted by a country's government.

pesticide—Product that kills insects or other organisms that would feed on or otherwise destroy crops.

plasmid—A ring of DNA whose structure lets it move readily into a cell.

promoter gene—Gene included in a DNA package to help express, or turn on, the gene for a desired trait.

recombinant DNA—DNA that combines genes from different sources.

resistance—Ability of an organism to survive a stress, such as an herbicide or pesticide.

For More Information

Government Agencies

United States Department of Agriculture
1400 Independence Avenue, S.W.
Washington, D.C. 20250
   202-264-8600

United States Environmental Protection Agency
1200 Pennsylvania Avenue, N.W.
Washington, DC 20460
   202-260-2090

United States Food and Drug Administration
5600 Fishers Lane
Rockville MD 20857
   888-INFO-FDA

Organizations

American Council on Science and Health
1995 Broadway, Second Floor
New York, NY 10023
   212-362-7044

Biotechnology Industry Organization
1625 K Street, N.W., Suite 1100
Washington, D.C. 20006
   202-857-0244

Center for Food Safety
666 Pennsylvania Avenue, S.E., Suite 302
Washington, D.C. 20003
   202-547-9359

Consumer Federation of America
1424 16th Street, N.W., Suite 604
Washington, D.C. 20036
   202-387-6121

Greenpeace International and Greenpeace USA
1436 U Street, N.W.
Washington, D.C. 20009
    800-326-0959

Grocery Manufacturers of America
1010 Wisconsin Avenue, N.W., 9th Floor
Washington, D.C. 20007
    202-337-9400

National Center for Food and Agricultural Policy
1616 P Street, N.W.
Washington, D.C. 20036
    202-328-5048

Organic Consumers Association
6114 Highway 61
Little Marais, MN 55614
    218-726-1443

Union of Concerned Scientists
2 Brattle Square
Cambridge, MA 02238
    617-547-5552

U.S. Public Interest Research Group
218 D Street, S.E.
Washington, D.C. 20003
    202-546-9707

Further Reading

Books

Anderson, Luke. *Genetic Engineering, Food, and Our Environment*. White River Junction, Vt.: Chelsea Green Publishing Co., 2000.

Cobb, Alan B. *Scientifically Engineered Foods: The Debate over What's on Your Plate*. New York: Rosen Publishing Group, 2000.

Greenhaven Staff. *Does Genetic Engineering Improve Agriculture?* San Diego, Calif.: Greenhaven Press, 1990.

Hawkes, Nigel. *Genetically Modified Foods*. Brookfield, Conn.: Millbrook Press, 2000.

Marshall, Elizabeth. *High-Tech Harvest*. Danbury, Conn.: Franklin Watts, 1999.

Tagliaferro, Linda. *Genetic Engineering: Progress or Peril?* Minneapolis, Minn.: Lerner Publishing Group, 1997.

Internet Addresses

United States Department of Agriculture
<http://www.usda.gov>

United States Environmental Protection Agency
<http://www.epa.gov>

Biotechnology Industry Organization
<http://www.bio.org/welcome.html>

Greenpeace
<http://www.greenpeace.org>

Index